The Wayside: Home of Authors

The Wayside in 1938

The Wayside: Home of Authors

Margaret M. Lothrop

American Book Company

New York   Cincinnati   Chicago
Boston   Atlanta   Dallas   San Francisco

This printing of *The Wayside: Home of Authors* is dedicated to the memory of its author, Margaret Mulford Lothrop who died in Concord, Massachusetts on May 14, 1970. She devoted the latter part of her life to the preservation of *The Wayside*. With great pleasure, she transferred the property with most of its furnishings to the Minute Man National Historical Park on June 22, 1965. The National Park Service now administers *The Wayside*.

Preface

My study of The Wayside history has been enriched through the courtesy and kindness of many persons. I am deeply indebted to the Boston Public Library for permission to quote from the Sophia Hawthorne Collection of Letters; and to Mr. Frederick Wolsey Pratt who kindly gave me access to diaries and letters of his great-grandparents, Mr. and Mrs. Amos Bronson Alcott, and of their daughter, Elizabeth. I have been graciously allowed to quote from the Journal kept by Nathaniel Hawthorne and his wife, 1844-1854, an Autograph Note for *Septimius Felton,* and a letter from Hawthorne to his wife, April 1, 1862, all in the Pierpont Morgan Library; nonsense verses composed by Hawthorne and his daughter, Una, owned by the Henry E. Huntington Library; a letter from Hawthorne to Duyckinck, June 15, 1852, in the Evert Augustus Duyckinck Collection of the New York Public Library; and a letter from Hawthorne to Franklin Pierce, July 5, 1852, owned by the New Hampshire Historical Society. For generous co-operation in making available to me the material of their proposed edition of Hawthorne's letters, I wish to thank Professor Stanley T. Williams of Yale University, Professor Randall Stewart of Brown University, Mr. Manning Hawthorne of the University of Maine, and Mr. Norman Holmes Pearson. Permission to publish Whittier's verse was kindly granted me by Mr. Greenleaf Whittier Pickard.

The late Mr. W. T. H. Howe, with his usual thoughtfulness, offered any of his manuscripts which might help me in my study. Four letters have been quoted in part: Hawthorne to William D. Ticknor, April 6, 1853; Hawthorne to his daughter, Rose, August 5, 1861; James Russell Lowell to Hawthorne, May 24, 1863; and Una Hawthorne to her aunt, Miss Elizabeth Palmer Peabody, June 5, 1861. Mr. Howe's untimely death has made the manuscripts temporarily inaccessible, so that in this case I have not been able to check the quoted passages with the originals.

For permission to use the pictures of the Alcott family and of "Hillside" I am indebted to the courtesy of Little, Brown, and Company. The Essex Institute, of Salem, Massachusetts, has kindly allowed me to reproduce the revealing portrait of Hawthorne by George P. A. Healey, painted almost immediately after the Hawthornes came to The Wayside in 1852. The Widener Library graciously made available the Harvard class picture of Julian Hawthorne. I am grateful to Mr. Richard C. Manning for permission to publish the photographs of Una and Rose Hawthorne. It is believed that these photographs and those of my mother are appearing in print for the first time.

Nor do I wish to forget my gratitude to the publishers, Houghton Mifflin Company and Little, Brown, and Company, who not only advised and helped me in the task of finding suitable material for illustrations but also freely gave me permission to quote from their books.

Others have helped me with encouragement and advice. I remember the kindly thoughtfulness of Professor Odell Shepard of Trinity College who facilitated access to certain important details. Two quotations in this book, taken from Mr. Alcott's diaries for February 9, 1847 and February 1, 1848, have already been published by Professor Shepard in *The Journals of Bronson Alcott* (pp. 190 and 202). For early encouragement, for information, and for continued interest in my task, I am especially grateful to Mr. Manning Hawthorne. Gracious courtesies have been received from Miss Belle da Costa Greene, librarian of the Pierpont Morgan Library, and from Mr. Leslie E. Bliss, librarian of the Henry E. Huntington Library. Patience and consideration have been shown by the staffs of the Manuscript and Rare Book Rooms of the various libraries, and especially by Miss Elizabeth Adams of the Boston Public Library. Innumerable courtesies, over a long period of time, have been extended to me by Miss Sarah R. Bartlett of the Concord Free Public Library, and by the members of her staff. Among those who have given me friendly advice and criticism are Miss Sarah A. Loomis, Mrs. Caleb Wheeler, Miss Marion A. Barker, and Dr. Miriam Thrall.

To each of these and to other friends who have aided me in this study, I take pleasure in expressing my sincere thanks.

MARGARET M. LOTHROP

Contents

PART I

The House Grown Old   3

PART II

Colonial Days and the Revolution   19

PART III

Hillside and the Alcotts   41

PART IV

Under Hawthorne's Many Roofs   79

PART V

The Lothrops and the Five Little Peppers   153

Chronologies 189   *Suggested Readings* 195   *Index* 199

Illustrated by
D. Putnam Brinley

Illustrations

The Wayside in 1938, Frontispiece

PART I

Front Hall. The Wayside Today, 8; Supposed Site of the Meeting Place of Septimius Felton and the British Soldier, 10

PART II

The Wayside as It Probably Looked in 1717, 20; Old North Bridge and Minute Man. About 1880, 34

PART III

Mrs. Amos Bronson Alcott, 40; Louisa May Alcott, 40; Amos Bronson Alcott, 40; Hillside about 1845. From an Old Drawing, 42; Steps Leading to the Terraces, 45; Colonial Fireplace in Southeast Bedroom, 47; Stairs Leading to the Attic Theater, 50

PART IV

Una Hawthorne, 78; Rose Hawthorne, 78; Nathaniel Hawthorne, 78; Julian Hawthorne, 78; Sophia Hawthorne, 78; The Wayside in 1853. After an Old Drawing, 83; Tower Study Showing Hawthorne's Standing Desk, 102; Mrs. Hawthorne's Parlor, Haw-

thorne's Armchair at Left, 105; Hawthorne's Seat on
the Hilltop. About 1880, 109; Hawthorne's Desk,
Bookcase, and Chair in Mrs. Hawthorne's Little
"Chapel," 129; The Wayside from the West. About
1885, 147

PART V

Mrs. Daniel Lothrop (as a young woman), 152; Mrs.
Daniel Lothrop (in later years), 152; Mr. Daniel
Lothrop, 152; Fireplace in the "Old Room." About
1900, 162; The Lothrop Sitting Room at the Way-
side, 174; Boulder at Foot of Hawthorne's Path.
Unveiled in 1904, 181; Home of Ephraim Wales
Bull with the Original Concord Grape Vine. About
1895, 184

I

The House
Grown Old

Many persons have asked me how this house happened to be the home of so many authors. It is true that eleven—if we include those who have published one book —have lived in The Wayside. By birth or marriage they were all connected with three families. Mr. and Mrs. Amos Bronson Alcott and their four daughters, later made famous in *Little Women,* lived here from April 1, 1845 to November 17, 1848. They were followed by Mr. and Mrs. Nathaniel Hawthorne and their relatives. The last author was my mother, Mrs. Daniel Lothrop, better known as "Margaret Sidney," who wrote *Five Little Peppers and How They Grew.*

When I tried to answer the question as to why the Alcotts and Hawthornes chose this particular house, I remembered that both families had previously lived in Concord, although at different periods of time. Each family, after an absence of a few years, had returned to the town where they had made many friends. This house, old even then, happened to be for sale when, in 1845, the Alcott family was in search of a home. By chance, several years later, the Hawthornes decided to buy at the time the Alcotts wished to sell.

The selection of The Wayside by my parents, Mr. and Mrs. Daniel Lothrop, was, however, a purposeful choice of Mr. Hawthorne's former home. It happened in this way. Early in 1883 they were boarding in Cambridge, Massachusetts, where they had lived most of the time since their marriage a year and a half earlier. They, too, wished to own a home, and had almost decided upon a

certain house on Brattle Street in Cambridge. One morning, when my father was on his way by streetcar to his
publishing office in Boston, he noticed a newspaper advertisement. It stated that the former home of Nathaniel
Hawthorne was for sale. Realizing immediately that his
wife would be entranced with the idea of owning such a
house, he interrupted his journey and stopped at the real-
estate office for the key and refusal. That night with
boyish enthusiasm he came up behind his wife and
dangled the key before her delighted eyes. Within a few
days they went to Concord to inspect the house. Well
satisfied, my father returned to the real-estate office to
complete the purchase. There he learned of the narrow
margin by which he had secured the property—hardly had
he left the office before a telegram came from Chicago,
ordering the firm to "hold The Wayside at any cost."

When my father and mother first came to The Wayside in 1883, it was, as it is today, a long rambling building of fifteen rooms and eight stairways; the piazza is the
only addition since that date. It was already a house of
many additions. Indeed its gradual development suggested to me one of my pet names for it, "Topsy." Like
the little colored girl, it "just grew." As a result there are
three distinct ridgepoles with as many different roof
lines. Surmounting all is the famous tower study built by
Mr. Hawthorne. In the middle of the building is the old
colonial two-story farmhouse of simple lines, its center

doorway now replaced by a bay window. On either side of this main part are two additions, or wings, set back a few feet from the front line of the house. In the western wing is still preserved the front door which the Hawthornes installed when they made their changes in 1860.

This old house, with colonial as well as literary associations, delighted my parents. Loving literature and history as they did, they determined to make as few changes as possible. They felt it a duty to preserve the physical structure as well as the fine traditions of the past, and they decided to repair, but not to change unless absolutely necessary. All that dated from the Hawthorne era was carefully saved, especially the wallpaper and the graining of the woodwork.

At the time my parents bought The Wayside, the exterior of the house badly needed paint. A rich buff, with cream trimmings, was chosen. Soon after the completion of the repairs, Mr. Julian Hawthorne returned to his childhood home to visit my parents. Standing in the road, and looking at the house, Mr. Hawthorne turned to my father and said, "Mr. Lothrop, how *did* you happen to choose that color? It is the exact shade I remember when I lived here as a boy." In 1932, nearly fifty years after that meeting, I saw Mr. Hawthorne in San Francisco. After a brief, but courteous, greeting he almost breathlessly said, *"Have* you changed the color of the old house?" He sighed with content when he was assured that the same shade had been kept and the home was little altered.

It must not be thought that the physical reminders of the past were the only, or chief, concern of my parents. They were deeply interested in the personalities and activities of the former owners. In fact, as I have stated, my father and mother were first drawn to the house because it had been the home of Nathaniel Hawthorne. His name was mentioned in our household almost as if he had been a close friend, although neither my father nor my mother had ever met him. Nevertheless he was always "Mr. Hawthorne," not the impersonal "Hawthorne" of books. Even now I can twist neither my tongue nor my pen to anything except "Mr. Hawthorne." It is as natural for me to speak of him in that way as it is for me to speak of other authors whom I did know, such as Mr. Whittier and Dr. Holmes. This attitude of respectful friendliness towards the former author-owners of our home is part of my earliest recollections, for I was born and brought up in The Wayside.

Toward the Hawthorne family there was a feeling of special friendliness. The younger daughter, Rose, then Mrs. George Parsons Lathrop, had become a firm friend of my mother, and often spent whole afternoons at The Wayside. She and my mother had first come to know each other when the Lathrops sold the house to my parents, but the chance acquaintanceship soon ripened into warm friendship. Mrs. Lathrop occasionally visited a cousin, Mrs. Mary Mann How, in the center of Concord, and almost invariably would come down to her old home, The Wayside, for a chat with this other author whose name was surprisingly like her own. On one such occasion Mrs. Lathrop climbed to her father's favorite path on top of the hill. From a pine tree near it she picked a branch which she brought back to the house. Later she painted for Mother a wooden fire screen, in soft shades of greens and browns, combining the pine branch with a quotation from her father's *Mosses from an Old Manse:*

FIRE WORSHIP

Beautiful it is to see the strengthening gleam, the deepening light that gradually casts distinct shadows of the human figure, the table and highbacked chairs upon the opposite wall, and at length, as twilight comes on, replenishes the room with living radiance and makes life all rosecolor.

Perhaps the article of furniture most prized by my mother was the mahogany dining table which had belonged to Mr. Hawthorne. She considered herself fortunate in being able to buy from Mrs. Lathrop this table and several other pieces of Hawthorne furniture, which were too bulky or otherwise unsuitable for a small

New York apartment. Among the other pieces were Mr. Hawthorne's red leather easy chair, his shaving stand, a bookcase, and bedroom chairs. Mrs. Lathrop told my mother that she was glad this furniture was to be used by an author and a publisher who would cherish it.

Front Hall
The Wayside Today

Since I was so well acquainted with Mrs. Lathrop, it was not strange that as a little girl, I should think of the other members of the Hawthorne family as personalities and not as mere names. I often wondered about them, and imagined how they had looked and acted. Yet they never appeared to me as ghosts. Perhaps I was spared that experience because of the death of my father when I was seven years old. He and I had been very close, our reactions being similar. To me he could never seem ghostlike; his spirit was far too vital. No more could I think of Mr. Hawthorne as a ghost. Yet I could easily picture him walking back and forth on the hillside, or climbing the stairs to his tower study. Sometimes the impression was so strong that I wished I could turn my head more quickly. Perhaps then, I liked to think, I might catch a glimpse of him starting up our front stairs.

The Alcott girls had lived in the house when they were children, and therefore were objects of my childhood imagination. I liked to think of them running through the rooms and along the terraces, and I often wondered whether they had had as good a time as I. At the age of four, I have been told, I used to climb up and down the winding colonial stairs, playing "Pilgrim's Progress" as Louisa and her sisters had done so many years before.

When I grew older and studied history, the colonial period also became vivid. It was not difficult to visualize the red coats and the muskets of the British soldiers who had marched past our house on their way to the Old North Bridge on April 19, 1775. Nor was it difficult to imagine the fight between the British officer and the young Concord man, which is supposed to have taken

*Supposed Site of the Meeting Place of
Septimius Felton and the British Soldier*

place on our hillside, according to a description by Mr. Hawthorne in *Septimius Felton*. Many times I have listened to my mother and watched her point out a spot on the hill where, tradition says, the British soldier was buried.

Fortunately for me, my imagination was not allowed to run riot. My mother possessed a sincere respect for historical accuracy, in addition to her ability for creative writing. Whenever she was composing an historical story she was attentive to even small details. I well remember one instance of her effort in that direction when she was writing *Little Maid of Concord Town*. In this story about the Revolutionary War she described the adventures of an imaginary Debbie Parlin and her family, placing them in an actual house, now "Grapevine Cottage." Among Debbie's friends was charming Millicent Barrett who really did live on Barrett's Mill Road. Shortly before the war Millicent had persuaded an admirer, a British officer, to teach her how to make a paper cartridge, a newly devised method for combining a bullet and gunpowder in the same container. Fortunately she had realized the value to the colonial cause of this invention which allowed a soldier to load his gun rapidly without measuring the powder between each shot. As soon as she could, Millicent gathered her girl friends, supposedly including Debbie, and taught them how to make the cartridges, which they, of course, turned over to their colonial officer friends. When Mother narrated this tale in *Little Maid of Concord Town*, she took pains to secure a picture of the scissors with which Millicent cut the paper for the cartridges, the scissors having been fortunately preserved in the Concord Free Public Library. As a young girl I was greatly impressed with the necessity for accuracy and vividness, for I was not only my mother's faithful reader, but her messenger, and I remember carrying many histories home on my bicycle from the library.

Another of Mother's characteristics was her deep interest in young people. Coupled with it was a sense of responsibility towards them. She believed that the heritage of the past should be preserved for their benefit. This belief ultimately led to the organization of the National Society, Children of the American Revolution, as I shall explain in a later chapter. It led her also to work for the preservation of historic houses, most notable of which was the Orchard House, where Louisa Alcott had accomplished much of her writing. So it was with The Wayside; Mother always welcomed to it groups of students and teachers. One of my very early memories is that of the Wellesley cheer, given by some jolly seniors as they departed after a visit to the house.

It was natural, therefore, when The Wayside came into my possession, that I should feel a responsibility for its future. I knew what it had done for me during my girlhood, in bringing history to life, and I wished that other young people might have the same joy. For them I decided to assemble all the interesting bits of information possible, about events, little as well as big, which had occurred in the house. Yet when I actually started the task I found that I did not know enough about the intimate family life of the Hawthornes and Alcotts. Unfortunately I was only a small girl, of about five years, when Mrs. Hawthorne's sister, Miss Elizabeth Palmer Peabody, the noted advocate of kindergartens, used to come to see Mother. I remember Miss Peabody's crown of white hair and commanding presence, but I was too young to have noticed what she may have said to my mother. Nor was I much older when Mrs. Rose Hawthorne Lathrop used to spend afternoons chatting with Mother.

I did not see Mrs. Lathrop again until 1924. In the meantime, after her husband's death, she had become Mother Mary Alphonsa of the Dominican Order, and had established Rosary Hill Home, a hospital for cancerous poor, in Hawthorne, New York, where I called upon her. Although far from well, she kindly came downstairs to talk with me. When she heard my plans for The Wayside, which she, too, had dearly loved, she said that she would write out for me some of her memories of her life there. Unhappily her death occurred two years later, before she had been able to put those memories on paper.

Her brother, Mr. Julian Hawthorne, I saw in 1932 in San Francisco, as I have mentioned. At that time he was erect in carriage and alert of mind although eighty-six years of age. He gave me a number of reminiscences of his boyhood in our home, and told me of the last time he had seen his father. As a freshman at Harvard College, he had gone to The Wayside to make some request of his father. After it had been granted and he was leaving the room, he glanced back at his father who was standing feebly by the bed, but gazing at him with an expression of particular affection.

To supplement these infrequent talks with Mrs. Lathrop and Mr. Julian Hawthorne I turned to manuscripts of letters and diaries written by the Hawthornes and Alcotts, and to certain personal papers of my mother. From these I have made many excerpts in order to give descriptions by actual observers. Among the more important items which I have found are the statements by my mother detailing how she happened to write *Five Little Peppers and How They Grew*, and why she chose the pen name of "Margaret Sidney." I found also a letter from Mrs. Hawthorne describing in a lively manner a dancing party she and her husband gave for their daughter Una. Quite as fortunate was the discovery of another letter, this time from Mrs. Alcott to her brother, in which she explained the repairs and changes which her husband and she made in the old colonial house shortly after they had bought it.

For still earlier periods of The Wayside history I have searched deeds and town records as well as family memoirs. Fortunately a descendant of the Whitneys, who were living in the house at the beginning of the Revolution, had compiled a narrative of the exciting events experienced in it on April 19, 1775. The town records of Concord also give many interesting bits of information about the various owners of the house in colonial times.

From all these sources I have found that The Wayside has been inhabited practically continuously since it was built about 1700, and all that time has been essentially a home. Its walls have resounded to the shouts of children. Within its rooms successive families have worked and played, have discussed world problems of the moment, and have made their contribution to the art of fine living.

During the two centuries of its existence, economic and political conditions changed radically. When the earliest part of the house was built, Massachusetts was an English colony, and remained so for seventy-five years. In that period ordinary life was vastly different from the hustling existence of the present. We of this generation can hardly picture its slow quality, the dangers and hardships involved, and the great amount of physical labor required to secure even food, shelter, and clothing. There were not even the conveniences which we now think of as necessities. There was no running water in the house, and in very cold weather the outdoor well had to be primed with hot water. Matches were unknown; if the fire went out recourse was to the tinder box, or to red-hot coals hastily carried on a shovel from a neighbor's house. The open fireplace with its oven was the only provision for cooking and heating. All the essentials for building a house, beams, planks, laths, nails, and other materials, were produced by hand labor. Transportation was still on horseback or by horse-drawn vehicles. It took a good part of a day to travel the twenty miles from Concord to Boston. The stage line was not started until 1791. The first postoffice in Concord was not opened until 1795.

Under these pioneer conditions, a member of the Ball family, about 1700, chose for his home a pleasant situation a mile from the center of town, close by the Bay Road which led from Concord to Boston. Protected from winter winds by a hillside on the north, the house faced south, its front rooms receiving sunshine all day long. Across the road the view over open fields was bounded by distant wooded hills.

Colonial Days
and the Revolution

T he Ball house was sturdily built. Its large central chimney, hand-hewn beams, "gunstock" posts—so called because of their shape—wooden pegs, and wide floor boards seem even now little affected by the passage of time. It was similar in plan to most of the farmhouses of the early colonial period. There were four sizable, low-ceilinged rooms, two above and two below, separated not only by the large center chimney, but also by a tiny entry, or passage way, on each floor. The stairs were steep and winding, occupying only half of the tiny entry space. Possibly there were at that time two additional rear rooms, both small, which were separated by their own chimney. One of these rooms was probably at the side of the house and therefore visible from the road. Although the date of the building of these rooms is uncertain, it is known that many years later the Alcotts combined two such rooms, a kitchen and a bedroom, into one large room which they used as a kitchen, but which is now called the "Old Room." Under its floor the remains of an old hearth can still be seen.

It is a great disappointment to me that as yet I have been unable to discover when the house was built. I have thoroughly searched town and county records of deeds, and even the probate records, returning more than once to be sure that I had not overlooked some hidden clue. In spite of my best efforts I have found nothing definite. The nearest date I can give is an approximate one, 1700; and for that the house itself is my authority. Certain structural details of the four main rooms and central chimney point to the latter part of the seventeenth or the very early part of the eighteenth century. Much older may have been the two small rooms at the rear of the main house; I am inclined to that belief because they had their own chimney. This arrangement of two rooms with a chimney between was a favorite one with the early settlers in Massachusetts.

Whatever the age of the house, it was built on part of an old "house lott," so called because on it were placed the owner's home, barn, and other farm buildings. In this section of Concord, the East Quarter, the first "house lotts" were set out on the slope of a long hill

*The Wayside as It
Probably Looked in 1717*

running eastward from Concord. These lots extended from the crest of the hill to the brook which flows through the meadow, an especially favorable location, protected from the north winds, yet open to the warmth of a southern exposure. It was not strange that in 1635, when the earliest settlers forced their way from Boston through heavy forests, they chose this slope for their crude shelters. For that first winter they built into the hillside in an effort to provide some sort of protection for their families. I have often looked at that hillside and marveled at the courage of those women and children who faced the cold of a New England winter under such almost unendurable conditions. As soon as possible tiny cabins were built at the foot of the hill, and these served until more permanent buildings could be erected. When the first road was made, it was laid out skirting the bottom of the hill in order to avoid both the marsh and the highland; a narrow space was left between the hill and the road for the houses. Opposite them, across the road, were built the barns.

The first divisions or assignments of land, soon after the founding of the town, were probably recorded with some degree of completeness. In 1666, however, the town felt it necessary to demand that all heads of families file a list of their holdings. At that time Nathaniel Ball, Sr., owned a "house lott" of thirteen acres. Twenty-two years later, one of his sons, Nathaniel, Jr., just three days before his marriage in 1688, received from his father the "unimproved half of the house lott," the remainder to go to him at his father's death.

The next date of which I am sure is nearly thirty years later, in 1717, when Caleb Ball, a son of this same Nathaniel, Jr., sold his home with three acres immediately surrounding it. With the date 1717, fortunately, my difficulties disappear. From that year to the present, the succession of deeds is complete. I wish, however, that I knew how Caleb came into possession of the property and when he came into the possession of it. I wish I knew whether it had a home on it when he secured it, or whether he himself built the comfortable house with its four main sunny rooms. In short, I wish I knew far more than the simple facts that this land was part of the original "house lott" of Nathaniel, Sr., and that the house which was upon it in 1717 is now, with its many additions, known as The Wayside.

At the time Caleb sold his property the house was in a fairly well settled community; some of the old houses which were close to it on either side have since then disappeared. As I thought of the life in such a community, I wondered what reasons had impelled Caleb to move his young family from the ancestral lands to a sparsely settled district where roads were poor and transportation both difficult and infrequent. His move was a complete one. He disposed not only of his house and its three acres, but also of his barn and eighteen additional acres of farming land, almost immediately buying a sixty-acre farm on the Lexington town line, some three or four miles from the center of Concord.

It must have taken a great deal of courage for Caleb and his wife Experience to leave their comfortable home in a closely settled community where they had many neighbors upon whom they could call in case of need. Only a stone's throw away towards the east was the home of Caleb's parents and their large family. Not far beyond was another house (now "Grapevine Cottage"). Within calling distance to the west of Caleb's house was the cottage of William Clark, and only a short distance beyond that was the Hoar home (now "Orchard House"). In these houses and in others nearby, many young people were living. Neighborhood entertainments, such as quilting parties or corn shuckings, would vary the monotony of the toil-laden days, and might be expected to appeal to Caleb and his wife. He was twenty-six and she a year younger when they took their two small daughters, the elder only two and a half years of age, to the distant farm.

Although Caleb was a young farmer to whom an increase in acreage might be attractive, that motive alone would presumably not account for the serious decision he had made. I was interested, therefore, to find that, at just about the same time, a number of other young farmers living along the Bay Road had left the center of Concord and bought large undivided farms on the outskirts, and I started to find out what changes taking place might have influenced Caleb and his fellows.

I learned that the lands which these young men were selling were neither easy nor profitable to till, partly because they were divided into scattered lots or "pieces," as they were described in the deeds. These often widely separated pieces were a natural outgrowth of the original division of Concord land. In addition to his "house lott" each head of a family was assigned a number of lots of farming land of various kinds, which generally included pasture, meadow, plowland, and woodland. In each assignment some good land and some poor land had been included. The purpose of such an arrangement had been, of course, to secure a distribution which would be fair to all; but the result had been an inconvenient scattering of any one person's holdings.

Although by 1717 there had been a change in ownership of individual lots, nevertheless the system prevailed, and it was difficult, or almost impossible, to buy enough contiguous lots to form a large farm near the center of town. Caleb had been caught by this system. The twenty-one acres which he sold were in four separate lots.

Fortunately by 1717 danger of the Indians attacking outlying farms was lessening. Through the persistence of the colonists, the Indians were being driven towards the western part of the state. King Philip's War, which had started in 1675, had brought real menace to the residents of Concord. Soldiers, at that time, were sent to help guard the town; garrison houses were built and homes were fortified, to which neighbors might go in case of alarm. Although the town of Concord was never attacked, yet in 1676 Indians captured a fifteen-year-old girl and killed her two brothers at Nashoba, a community then within the limits of Concord, but some seven miles from the center of town. This tragedy occurred in spite of the fact that the young men had posted their sister on a nearby hill to warn them of any approach of Indians, while they threshed grain in their barn. Although she later made her escape, inhabitants of other towns not far from Concord were not so fortunate. Dunstable, Groton, and Lancaster, as Shattuck mentions in his well-known history of Concord, "were often attacked by Indians from 1694 to 1712, and many of the inhabitants were killed or carried into captivity."[1] He adds that raids were made even on Chelmsford and Sudbury. A Major Tyng, for instance, was fatally wounded by Indians in 1711 as he was traveling between Groton and Concord, but he managed to reach Concord before his death. As a result of these conditions some of the Concord men were constantly employed as scouts, or were detailed to garrison houses or forts.

[1] Lemuel Shattuck, *A History of the Town of Concord* (1835), p. 66.

When the outlying farms became safe, the effects of Concord's system of land division would have been far more serious for the progressive farmers had they not been able to sell at a good price their town homes and land. Fortunately for them some of the young men were beginning to turn from farming as a vocation and were becoming artisans, encouraged by a growing demand for objects and services which required specialized skill. In most instances these artisans continued to do a small amount of farming, enough to provide for their own needs, and were therefore glad to buy houses which had a small acreage of farming land near the center of town.

This increased demand for the products of artisans particularly attracted my attention because it seemed to mark the development of Concord from a frontier community to a settled town where fears for personal safety were giving way to considerations of leisure, comfort, and beauty. The rise of an enterprising man was sometimes rapid. For instance, Samuel Fletcher, Jr., to whom Caleb Ball sold his house and land, was at the time of the transaction, a simple glazier. Only five years later, when this same Samuel Fletcher in his turn sold his home, he had become a builder and planner of houses, giving his occupation as that of "housewright."

As it happened the Ball house, which Samuel Fletcher had bought from Caleb Ball in 1717 and which he sold in 1722 to Nathaniel Colburn, continued for over fifty years to be the home of specialists of one sort or another. For twenty-four of those years Nathaniel Colburn, another "housewright," made it his home and in it brought up his large family. The next owner, John Breede, was a cordwainer, that is, a worker in leather, or a shoemaker. The third man, a "trader," was Samuel Whitney, who occupied the house from 1769 to 1776. An able and intelligent patriot, he was destined to take a stirring part in the events leading up to the Revolution.

Life during those fifty years flowed on fairly prosperously in the old house. Many children filled its rooms, and I like to think how its walls must have resounded to their laughter and the clatter of their heels. There must have been much noise and hilarity because in the Colburn family, for instance, there were eleven children, all except one of whom were born in the house. The Breedes had ten children. When the Whitneys sold the house and moved to Boston, they had eleven. Those were days of large families, four more children being born to the Whitneys in later years.

The owners of the house took their share in the life of the town, serving in the various offices to which they were elected. The old town records show that Nathaniel Colburn was often chosen to be one of the "Horse Officers" and "Field Drivers," or "Haywards," as Shattuck describes the latter term. John Breede, as his vocation might suggest, was frequently elected one of the three "Sealers of Leather." Occasionally he was chosen for other offices, such as tithingman, fence viewer, or surveyor of the highway. As can be seen from these titles, careful supervision was maintained by the town over the quality of private goods offered for sale, as well as over the general condition of the town itself. For instance, certain men were appointed to take care of stray animals, especially horses, when the court met in Concord, and certain others were named to see that private fences were kept mended. It is amusing to find that for many years a vote was taken at each annual town meeting to determine whether swine should be allowed to run free in the streets.

These and other town records show that the early owners of the house were men of parts. Nathaniel Colburn, for example, would seem to have been a trusted workman since through many consecutive years his name appears frequently when he was paid for repairs on the meeting house, the schools, and the homes of the poor for whom the town was responsible. He was apparently a man who knew his own mind, being in 1724 one of only fourteen men to dissent from a certain vote at a town meeting. Yet he must have been respected and well liked, because he was made in 1747 a member of a committee of five, selected to consider what measures might properly be taken to "promote peace and unanimity, in the first precinct."

Only a year earlier he, or perhaps his twenty-three year-old son, was corporal in a company of fifty men, who on September 23, 1746 were "detached and marched to Boston on an alarm, on account of an expected attack from the French fleet under the Duke D'Anville."[2] To be sure, the company was away from Concord only ten days, but at that time such a march was notable. It must have been an interesting and valuable experience for the men, since trips to Boston could not have been of frequent occurrence. There was no stagecoach line, roads were poor, and the amount of time required by the journey could not generally be spared from work at home.

The trader Samuel Whitney, most important among the early owners of the house, was one of the leaders in town affairs during the momentous period immediately preceding and following the fight of April 19, 1775. He was a forceful man, a firm believer in liberty, and well connected in Boston through influential relatives and friends. His earlier commercial ventures in that city as a "trader" had been practically wrecked by depreciating currencies, the bankruptcies of various firms, and the decreasing trade with England. In 1767 he moved to Concord and in the next few years bought much property, helped by an inheritance from his mother. In 1769 he purchased John Breede's house and made it his home. He

[2] Shattuck, *op. cit.*, p. 71.

bought also a small house next door, which had been built about 1740. This he probably made into the country store or shop which he is known to have started about this time. This shop was mentioned later by a British spy in a report to General Gage who ordered his officers to search particularly the Whitney buildings.

Samuel Whitney's ability was at once recognized in Concord, and he was elected to important offices. He was made Muster Master of the Concord Minute Men, one of the three delegates to the Provincial Congress, and a member of many committees, especially those of Safety and Correspondence. In this last capacity he was particularly valuable, since he could secure early information from his friends and relatives in Boston, and discuss with them the serious situation when they came to visit him in Concord.

Thoughtful men foresaw that the rising opposition to British tyranny would lead to drastic action, possibly to fighting. It was recognized that, in such an event, large stores of weapons, bullets, powder, and provisions would be necessary. On October 24, 1774, at a town meeting of which Samuel Whitney was moderator, Concord voted that supplies of cannon ball, grape shot, and powder be purchased for the cannon which the Committee of Safety had brought into the town. Other public stores were collected and entrusted to those persons who were known to be workers for liberty, Samuel

Whitney himself receiving eighty-two barrels of flour and other articles. British spies, however, visited Concord and reported to General Gage the location of many of the hiding places. By one of these spies Samuel Whitney was accused of concealing arms and ammunition.

Fortunately for the defenders of liberty, word came from Boston that General Gage was considering sending an expedition to capture the supplies. Many of the stores, including those entrusted to Mr. Whitney, were hurried into more secure hiding places or moved to other towns, even as far as Shirley.

The day of April 19, 1775 was one long to be remembered by Mr. Whitney, his wife, and children, as we learn from the Whitney family account, a valuable record since it was compiled in 1860 from memoranda preserved in the various branches of the family. It states that before daybreak the household was aroused by a near neighbor, young Dr. Samuel Prescott, who hurriedly told them of the approach of the British troops and of his own fortunate escape from a British patrol. Although the Whitney account does not give the details of his ride, we know from Shattuck's *History of Concord* that Dr. Prescott had "spent the evening at Lexington, at the house of Mr. Milliken, to whose daughter he was paying his addresses." Hearing of the alarm in Lexington, Dr. Prescott had hurried towards home and had overtaken Paul Revere and William Dawes, who were then on their way to warn Concord. Traveling with them and helping them to spread the alarm at the farmhouses they passed, Dr. Prescott managed to escape when the other two men were stopped by an advance guard of the British.

After hearing Dr. Prescott's alarming news, Samuel Whitney hurriedly dressed and hastened off, "gun in hand" to warn others, but not before he had cautioned his wife to remain at home and to keep the children indoors. Fortunately most of the flour which had been stored by Mr. Whitney had already been moved to a safer place. There was much, however, for him to do in consulting with the other leaders, as well as in sending out further warnings and in making a few last minute shifts of the stores hidden in Concord.

Mrs. Whitney and her family were not long left in peace. The Lincoln Minute Men, aroused by messengers sent by Dr. Prescott, came hurrying down the lane which meets the highway nearly in front of the house. Rumors flew thick and fast about the happenings in Lexington. Soon came the sound of drums and fifes; the British soldiers were marching close by the house, the Grenadiers on the road in front, the Infantry on the hill behind.

The Whitney boys wanted to follow the British soldiers, but their mother threatened them with severe punishment if they left the house without her permission, and warned them of "their father's displeasure, which they well knew was not to be incurred with impunity."[3] In spite of her admonition thirteen-year-old David could not resist temptation and disappeared from home to the consternation of his family.

The anxious morning wore on. Suddenly Mr. Whitney came running down the hillside, having cut across the fields after the fight at the Old North Bridge. He said that the family must leave at once, since he feared that the house might be entered by the aroused British soldiers when they passed on their return to Boston. The homes of those active in colonial affairs were known, many of them having been visited; and threats had been made against the owners. In addition the British soldiers had started to burn public buildings. The older Whitney children were therefore hastily sent to a distant part of Concord, and Mrs. Whitney with four of the youngest boys—all under five years of age—was bundled into the country chaise, a high-wheeled carriage. They had proceeded but a short distance toward Bedford when a bullet went through the top of the chaise, grazing the head of the four-year-old boy. They were not further molested, however, and were hindered only by innumerable questions from the Minute Men of other towns, who were hurrying to join in the pursuit of the British.

[3] *Incidents in the Life of Samuel Whitney* . . . Collected by his great-grandson, Henry Austin Whitney (1860), p. 28.

Late in the afternoon, after the sound of the firing had died down, Mrs. Whitney and the children returned to their home, to be greeted by David and his father, both of whom were unharmed. David, who had frightened his family by his disappearance in the morning, had calmly watched the fight at the bridge from a hill on the north side of the river, taking good care, however, to keep well out of his father's sight. He told his family that it never occurred to him that there was real danger, until he heard the whistling of the bullets. Then he hastily made good his escape and ran home.

*Old North Bridge and
Minute Man. About 1880*

The Whitneys lived in Concord until shortly after the evacuation of Boston by the British, when they moved to the city to be near relatives. David, however, was apparently attracted by country life, because he remained in Concord and was apprenticed to a farmer, Thaddeus Hunt. After attaining his majority, David, too, moved away, though he later returned on the occasion when he claimed a bride.

This short account of the Whitney family is incomplete without reference to a Negro slave of theirs, named Casey. In his early life he had had a bitter experience, for he had been captured in Africa when he was only twenty years old and brought to America, leaving behind his wife and child. Casey declared that each night he went home to Africa, returning in the morning. Henry D. Thoreau, commenting upon this homesick dream, in his diary under date of February 18, 1858, described the later adventures of Casey. It seems that one Saturday while Casey was chopping wood in the yard, one of the Whitney boys kept throwing snowballs at him. At last Casey, annoyed beyond control, hurled his ax at the lad. Whereupon, Samuel Whitney, the father, told Casey that he was an "ugly nigger" and threatened him with jail. The following Sunday Casey ran away, pursued by neighbors across the Great Meadows, which lay behind the Whitney hillside. He reached the river in safety and managed to hide himself in it, keeping his face only above water. After dark he secured food from a kindly woman and then betook himself far away. He enlisted and, after the war had ended, was given his freedom in return for his military service.

Although the Whitneys moved to Boston in 1776, their old house was not sold until 1778. It then became the home of a prosperous farmer, Daniel Hoar (who had been born in a neighboring house, now known as "Orchard House"), and later of his son, Daniel, Jr. The latter planned to bring to it his bride, Mary Adams; but his plans, after all preparations had been made, even to the completion of the wedding dress, came to a tragic end by his accidental drowning in Flint's Pond (now Sandy Pond).

After a few years Daniel's heirs, his brothers and sisters, sold the property to a wheelwright, Darius Merriam, of Concord. One of its small buildings he utilized as his shop, and in it turned out wheels, in the laborious fashion necessary before steam-driven machinery came into general use. He and his wife and two sons lived in the house for only a few years before he sold it to Horatio Cogswell, also a wheelwright. During the latter's ownership it was mortgaged to Albert Lawrence Bull, a cabinet maker, who is said to have lived in it. His brother, Ephraim Wales Bull, came to Concord that same year, 1836, and bought the neighboring place (now "Grapevine Cottage"). On its surrounding acres Mr. Bull, by trade a goldbeater, originated the Concord grape, now so famous. He was an interesting man of an original turn of mind, who, as we shall see, became the friend of Nathaniel Hawthorne and of other owners of The Wayside. I remember gratefully his kindness to us neighborhood children, when years later he used to give us grapes and roses, or allow us to wander in his greenhouse.

In 1845 the old house again changed hands, this time to become the home of one of Concord's most famous families, the Alcotts. The house was indeed an old one now. It had stood at least 130 years, through the town's colonial period, the War for Independence, and the early years of the republic. Yet for it the date 1845 marked the beginning of a new type of pioneer life.

Hillside and the Alcotts

MRS. ALCOTT

LOUISA MAY ALCOTT

AMOS BRONSON ALCOTT

The turmoil and strife of meeting frontier conditions and of wresting political liberty had passed, but there was still turmoil and strife in men's minds. Liberty of thought and the sanctity of individual life were pressing questions. To the old house which had sheltered pioneers of the early days came other leaders, prophets of a richer intellectual life. One of the foremost of these was Amos Bronson Alcott. A philosopher, with a tender love for all defenseless creatures, he could not endure the shackles of the educational system of that day. He was a pioneer, indeed, for an education that should fit the individual for the joy of independent thought.

To the old house, on April 1, 1845, came this philosopher, his wife, and his four daughters, Anna, Louisa, Elizabeth, and Abba May, better known to us as Meg, Jo, Beth, and Amy in *Little Women*. They were very happy; at last a home of their own! Not only did they appreciate the comfort and space of a whole house, after renting rooms; even more, they enjoyed the sense of ownership and the hope of permanency.

The last two years had not been very happy ones for the Alcotts. In the summer and fall of 1843, they had been members of the group which conducted the unfortunate experiment in community living at Fruitlands, in Harvard, Massachusetts. From Harvard they had moved to Still River, and then, to their great pleasure, they had returned to Concord, and their old friends. Even then, in spite of the kindness of Mr. and Mrs. Edmund

Hosmer, in whose house on Sandy Pond Road they had rented rooms, they were not entirely contented. They wanted their own home and an opportunity to support themselves adequately.

It was, therefore, a real joy to them to be able to buy a house and land. Mrs. Alcott had been a beneficiary under the will of her father, Colonel Joseph May of Boston. Since the estate had been distributed in the preceding August, part of Mrs. Alcott's share could now be used in purchasing the old Cogswell house, with its adjacent buildings, and an acre of land. Eight acres of especially fertile land across the highway were bought at the same time by the Alcotts' good friend, Ralph Waldo Emerson, and loaned to them.

Hillside about 1845. From an Old Drawing

Both to Mr. Alcott and to his family, the new property, which they named "Hillside," meant spiritual as well as physical well-being. To all of them it gave sufficient space in which they could comfortably maintain their family life, freed from too great proximity to others. To Mr. Alcott, who was forty-five years old, it gave opportunity, by tilling the soil, to contribute to the support of his family. Idealistic as he was and eager to be intellectually of service to the world, he nevertheless accepted the manual labor involved in this new opportunity and was thankful for relief from the discouragement of the preceding months.

He had not always been so helpless. In the early eighteen-thirties, he had had a school in Germantown and another in Philadelphia. In 1834 he opened the famous Temple School in Boston, which he conducted in the face of various difficulties until 1839. Although he had a real contribution to make to the progress of education, unfortunately for him and for the pupils of that day, his ideas seemed radical to their parents. He believed that education should be made interesting to young people and that it should stimulate and exercise their powers of observation and of analysis. This training in independent thinking was directly opposed to the educational principles of his day. Parrot-like memorizing of facts was all that was considered necessary, any deficiency on the part of the student being remedied by the application of the rod. Mr. Alcott and his friend, Henry David Thoreau, who taught the town school in Concord for a few weeks following his graduation from Harvard in 1837, did not agree with these principles and objected to the use of the ferule, even at the risk of losing their schools.

This courageous adherence to his convictions Mr. Alcott never lost. When in 1839 it came to the point of closing his Temple School in Boston, or of denying admission to a clean little colored girl, he chose the former alternative, loyal to his belief in equality of opportunity for all. The parents of his other scholars, already antagonistic, soon withdrew their support from his school.

Since Mr. Alcott could no longer utilize his intellectual ability in his favorite vocation, he determined to turn all of his powers to the physical task of farming this land which so providentially had been made available to him. His diaries describe, day by day, his hard manual work in preparing the earth, planting and tending his beds, and finally harvesting the crops. The list of his vegetables and fruits would be almost endless. Squash, cucumbers, lettuce, peas, beans, potatoes, beets, radishes, celery, tomatoes, corn, spinach, turnips, rhubarb, strawberries, quince, currants, apples, peaches, pears, buckwheat, and rye are some of them. Nor did he forget flower beds. Work in the soil was not new to him; he was a farmer's boy and had learned not only to plant and tend, but also to love all growing things. His was a mind which saw grandeur in simplicity, beauty in all forms of nature, and joy in truth, gentleness, and duty.

Although he always preferred to teach, he was glad that he had this farming ability which now led him to

Steps Leading to
Terraces behind the House

outdoor tasks. In these tasks his daughters often joined him, helping him to plant peas and beans, or to weed and keep neat the rows of vegetables or the garden paths. Elizabeth was the one most apt to help him, although Louisa also often worked manfully at the task. On one or more occasions Mrs. Alcott assisted him in setting out apple trees. The orderly arrangement of his garden across the road and, later, of the terraces behind the house was a source of great pleasure to him. His love of beauty challenged as well as recompensed. To him the creation of beauty in nature was a step toward God. In his diaries Mr. Alcott often rejoiced that he could bring order and beauty to this new "estate," as he affectionately called it.

Inside the house Mrs. Alcott planned the necessary changes. There was much to be done to repair the old house and to enlarge it. Mr. N. Hosmer, the carpenter, found that the wheelwright's shop was still sturdy and could be utilized. This small building was therefore cut in two, one part being added to each end of the house. The western addition, or wing, now provided a study for Mr. Alcott, as well as two small rooms on the first floor, the half story above having space for two or more additional rooms.

The better half of the shop, Mrs. Alcott wrote to her brother, Samuel J. May, was moved up to the eastern end of the building and converted into a bath-house and a woodhouse. She told of arrangements for "bathing tub and shower bath fixed with weight and pullies so that even Elizabeth can give herself a bath without help." This arrangement was a great accomplishment, almost a radical innovation, at a time when the physical difficulties of obtaining water from wells, combined with the usual custom of the Saturday night bath, conspired to keep from daily bathing all but the most devoted believers in cleanliness.

Mrs. Alcott added that they had built new stairs to the children's room; this was the southeast bedroom

Colonial Fireplace and
Closet Door in Southeast Bedroom

where "the east grows rosy with the coming day," as Louisa wrote in *Little Women* when describing the books which the girls found under their pillows on Christmas morning. The room is an interesting one, with its old colonial fireplace and the four corner "gunstock" posts which date back to Caleb Ball's time or earlier. Hidden behind hand-split laths and old plaster over the fireplace is some "shadow molded" vertical sheathing of that very early era. Behind the sheathing is a space which may have been used as a hideaway; certain recent discoveries point to that possibility. Perhaps Samuel Whitney utilized the space in 1775 for the concealment of colonial stores. It would have made a good hiding place for the escaped slave to whom the Alcotts gave protection in 1847. At that later date Louisa and her sisters had separate rooms in the western addition, but in 1845, when they first came to the house, this big southeast room was their bedroom.

Downstairs greater comfort was secured by combining the two small rooms at the rear of the house. Mrs. Alcott wrote that the little bedroom was moved to the west side of the old kitchen and intervening partitions were taken down. The large room thus formed was used by the Alcotts as their kitchen. Mrs. Alcott went on to say: "I have had the water brought into the kitchen and a new pump—had the well cleaned out and stoned round it." Full of enthusiasm she added that they were beginning on the fence, an examination having shown that its posts were nearly gone and that it was "in a state of decay throughout." Not daunted by the hard work, she wrote happily:

> We are getting through with our repairs as well as we could hope—and begin to find a comfort which I had not realized in my most sanguine hopes.

This sense of enjoyment in their new home was shared by the girls, who were of the age to find adventure and pleasure in everything. Anna, the "Meg" of *Little Women*, had just had her fourteenth birthday. Twelve-year-old, long-legged, active Louisa, "Jo," was a joy to all with her ever-ready fund of jollity. Lovable "Beth" was nine years of age; and roly-poly Abba May, "Amy," with blue eyes and golden hair, the pet of the whole family, was only four years old. Their mother wrote:

> My girls are doing well, Louisa enjoying the season—weeds with her father like a Trojan—Anna sticks to the books—and Elizabeth is smiling on every thing as if love was as cheap as dirt.

To the girls the old house, with its big attic, the barn, and the steep hillside at the rear were all special playgrounds. The barn won their particular regard. It served as a wonderful theater in which they could perform the exciting and romantic plays which Louisa created either from the fairy stories which they all knew, or from her imaginings about the adventures of cavaliers and their ladies. The hayloft became a particularly advantageous spot from which to lower the bag with the black pudding to rest on the nose of the old witch; or to which Jack the Giant Killer could climb. The large colonial attic was sometimes their theater; at other

Stairs Leading to the Attic Theater

times it served for rainy day games, or, when life became too strenuous, for a quiet retreat where one could
read and eat an apple.

One of their diversions was to listen to a story, and
then to enact what they had heard. Christian, in *Pilgrim's
Progress*, was a favorite character whose adventures they
imitated. Louisa has described in *Little Women* the girls'
journeys on the terraces, through the house, and up to
the flat roof—the "Celestial City,"—where they "sang
for joy in the sunshine."

Life was not all fun for the Alcott girls. For all
their high spirits, they obeyed a regular routine which
included time for household duties, for worship, and
for conversation, as well as for play. Bronson Alcott,
thought by many to be an impractical philosopher, had
a keen sense of orderliness. Often in his diary he made a
"Day's Order" for himself at the beginning of a month,
outlining the various duties or other activities of a
representative day. A similar "Day's Order" was frequently written for the girls, outlining their activities,
the hours varying somewhat with the seasons. In winter
the family rose at six, but in summer at five; an hour
later came breakfast, time being allowed for bathing
and dressing. At breakfast Mr. Alcott read from the
Bible, discussed with them some problems of the day,
and then they would all join in singing hymns, while
Mrs. Alcott played the piano, "Seraphene." This little

service was not formal; it was adapted to even the youngest, and was enjoyed by all. Mr. Alcott often mentioned in his diary the effect of a particular scripture reading or hymn upon one or another of the girls; sometimes Beth discussed the reading with him, sometimes one of the girls copied a verse in her journal.

The morning was filled with household tasks in which the girls helped their mother, after which there was a short recreation period, preceding two hours of study with their father. The noon dinner was followed by recreation, and by hours set aside for sewing, reading, and conversation with their mother. After supper there was reading aloud, or music, and other recreation, preceding an early bed hour. In the schedule plenty of time was allowed for games and for individual amusement of all kinds; yet each person's responsibility to share in the family work and pleasure was stressed. Beth, in her diary in 1846, just before her eleventh birthday, speaks almost daily of cleaning the knives and from time to time of ironing, of sweeping the sitting room and washing the hearth, or of washing the dishes.

An important part of the instruction which Mr. Alcott gave to his daughters was the composition and writing of a diary. Beth has stated that she first wrote her record of the day's events on a slate. After showing it to her father, she copied the corrected version in her Journal, using pen and ink. The parts of her Journal which have been preserved show her careful and beautiful penmanship.

During a good part of their stay at Hillside Mr. Alcott taught his girls for two hours a day. Beth in her diary often mentioned her pleasure in the lessons, giving examples of her drawing and arithmetic, or of some poem she had learned. Her father's conversational method is exemplified in some of her remarks about her geography lesson, when she wrote "we talked about" Rhode Island, or Massachusetts, as the case might be. He believed in making a geography lesson practical, and by way of illustration drew a map of Rhode Island for Beth in her diary. Louisa, in a sketch written in later years for a friend, has spoken appreciatively of her father's instruction.

Life was by no means all study and work for the Alcott girls. Beth describes many simple pleasures: going with their father to "Walden Wood" for trees to plant in their front yard, walking or sitting on the hill behind their home where they would make flower wreaths for their heads and enjoy the sunset or a rainbow. Often their mother was persuaded to leave her household duties and join the group.

Always ready for a lark and companionship, the girls had many friends among their neighbors. Beth frequently mentions Ellen and Edith Emerson, the Hosmer sisters, Cary Moore, Johnny and Warren Bull next door, and others with whom they visited back and forth. Usually these friends came for an afternoon's play, but sometimes there was a special celebration, such as a birthday party. Although such anniversaries were always remembered in the Alcott family, the entertainment generally took the form of asking two or three friends to join the family at their midday dinner or at supper. Beth's twelfth birthday, however, was made a special occasion, the scene being the arbor which her father had built on the hillside. Mr. Alcott, in writing of Beth in his diary, June 24, 1847, described the party:

> It was celebrated in the evening, by lights in the arbour, music, and some *tableau*, arranged by her mother and sisters, and to which her little friends from the village were invited. The effect was very pretty, and gave infinite satisfaction to the little company.

Simplicity was the keynote of the Alcott girls' activities, whether in their special entertainments or in their usual occupations. Their games, for instance, were generally taken from their own experiences, such as Going to Boston, Sick Lady, or the perennial one, School. They were active children: Beth often mentions a run in the garden, or down a steep hill, or a sprint to the brook with Louisa, who was quite equal to successful competition with the boys. A neighbor, Clara Gowing, writing of her girlhood memories in *The Alcotts as I Knew Them*, has described Louisa when she was thirteen as "tall and slim," adding "she was the fleetest runner in school, and could walk, run and climb like a boy." [1] Yet with all their love of activity and companionship, the girls liked to be by themselves, writing or reading.

Louisa was an interesting combination of varied abilities, energies, and interests. Mrs. Alcott understood the warring factors in her daughter's temperament, and realized that loving and tender care was needed to help her to the full and happy development of her unusual gifts. Mrs. Alcott, therefore, encouraged her in her writing of poetry as an outlet for her emotions. The last verse of the poem "Despondency" [2] which she wrote at Hillside in August, 1845, when she was twelve, shows the triumph of her courage.

> *Then why be sad*
> *When all are glad,*
> *And the world is full of flowers?*
> *With the gay birds sing,*
> *Make life all Spring,*
> *And smile through the darkest hours.*

The "gentle, persevering discipline" of Mr. Alcott, as his wife once described it, and the affection, high

---

[1] Clara Gowing, *The Alcotts as I Knew Them* (1909), p. 6.

[2] Ednah D. Cheney (ed.), *Louisa May Alcott, Her Life, Letters and Journals* (1889), p. 44.

ideals, and religious faith with which the Alcott girls were surrounded in their home, are seen in another poem, "My Kingdom," which Louisa wrote during that same August. This poem, with many quotations from Louisa's diaries and letters, has been published by Mrs. Ednah D. Cheney in *Louisa May Alcott, Her Life, Letters and Journals.* In the same book are quotations from Louisa's sketch of her childhood in which she described her "romantic period," when she was fifteen and loved to walk in the moonlight. It was during these girlhood years at Hillside that Louisa was first allowed to browse among Mr. Emerson's books, curled up in a comfortable chair in his study.

The Alcott girls' problems were closely watched by their mother who was privileged to read their diaries. Often she would slip a word of encouragement or of caution under a pillow or in a journal. At one time when Louisa was longing for a room of her own, her mother urged her to be patient. When her obedience was later rewarded, she wrote jubilantly in her journal:

March, 1846, — I have at last got the little room I have wanted so long, and am very happy about it. It does me good to be alone, and mother has made it very pretty and neat for me. My work-basket and desk are by my window, and my closet is full of dried herbs that smell very nice. The door that opens into the garden will be very pretty in summer, and I can run off to the woods when I like.

I have made a plan for my life, as I am in my teens and no more a child. I am old for my age, and don't care much for girl's things. People think I'm wild and queer; but mother understands and helps me. I have not told any one about my plan; but I'm going to *be* good. I've made so many resolutions, and written sad notes, and cried over my sins, and it doesn't seem to do any good! Now I'm going to *work really,* for I feel a true desire to improve, and be a help and comfort, not a care and sorrow, to my dear mother.[3]

It is thought that four small rooms in the western addition, two of which were on the ground floor, and two in the attic, were arranged for the children at this time. Louisa was evidently given one of the lower rooms since she mentioned in her diary the door opening into the garden, and the ease with which she could run into the woods.

All of the family enjoyed the woods, and often went to walk in them. The children, occasionally accompanied by their mother, loved to go with their father to find spruce, larch, and other trees, which they brought from Walden Woods or from the hill behind the house.

3 Cheney, *op. cit.,* p. 44.

Although only part of the steep slope was included in the purchase of the house, Mr. Alcott leveled and sodded terraces on the lower part, set out peach and apple trees, and with the help of a neighbor constructed a stone wall behind the barn. He arranged winding paths and rustic fences in order to give the proper setting for the various small buildings which he constructed: a bee house, and what he spoke of as a conservatory, for early vegetables. Yet always he looked longingly at the hilltop from which, as he wrote in his diary, there was "a commanding view of the valley of the brook and its serpentine windings through the meadows. . . . " He added:

> . . . my garden is seen to great advantage from its top. I should like to build a *Lodge* there. There is already some shrubbery of pines and birches, and spruce and larch might easily be transplanted. The level plain [place?] above would be a fine scite [*sic*] for an orchard of peaches free from the early frosts of spring and summer.

Great was his pleasure when, late in 1846, his brother-in-law, Samuel J. May, bought three acres including the hilltop and allowed Mr. Alcott to include the new purchase in the Hillside property.

Among the rustic structures with which he adorned this "estate," the most ambitious was an arbor, or summer house, on one of the terraces. As with the other rustic buildings, he secured from the woods most of his materials for this arbor, small trees, osiers, or twisted branches whose curves particularly appealed to his fancy, so that he was obliged to buy only a comparatively small amount of lumber. The work was a gratification of his strong creative instinct. He made lattices of hemlock and willow, built eight gables, erected columns for a portico and floored the arbor, then thatched the roof with straw from the rye which he had grown and threshed. Finally, accompanied by Mrs. Alcott and Elizabeth, he returned from the woods with running pine and plush moss for the decoration of the seat and Gothic columns. The family was keenly interested in the progress of the arbor, and visited it each evening before supper. It was used for many occasions: Beth's birthday, as has already been mentioned, was celebrated in it with tableaux; Louisa in her description of her childhood wrote:

> . . . strawberry parties in the rustic arbor were hon-
> ored by poets and philosophers, who fed us on their
> wit and wisdom while the little maids served more
> mortal food.[4]

Mr. Alcott's creative desires were not satisfied by the terraces and rustic buildings on the hillside. In the space between the house and the road, pines and spruce were transplanted. Across the road in the garden plot he

---

[4] Cheney, *op. cit.*, p. 31.

planted willows, which he trimmed. Many apple trees were set out, both on the terraces and in the garden. Paths were arranged in a manner, which, as he remarked with pleasure, "enhanced the view from the hilltop." His most important arrangement in this part of the grounds was a semicircular ditch which carried a stream to a little reservoir, or basin, at the foot of the pump, and then back to the brook near the bridge over which the lane leading to Lincoln passed. To make the reservoir more convenient for bathing in summer, he built a small house over it. The following entry in his diary shows how much thought had gone into the planning:

> Over this basin, I mean to build a neat rustic structure, for Bathing, and an alcove for retreating from the summer heat and rains. The field at present, is without character, a bald plain, it needs some object of art to give a central point, around which other objects shall be grouped. This building will stand in the center of my garden and will be altogether a pretty spectacle from all points.

When the Garden House was nearly completed, he wrote that the columns of the piazza "have the effect of the most costly carved work; and the colouring, of spruce and willow interspersed, is inimitable by art."

These rustic additions to his estate were the object of curiosity in the village. Neighbors would stop to look and comment. Among those particularly interested was Mr. Emerson who had originally provided the eight-acre garden plot for Mr. Alcott's use. From the very beginning of the Hillside enterprise Mr. Emerson had encouraged his friend's efforts. The rustic arbor particularly pleased him, so much so that the following summer, 1847, he commissioned Mr. Alcott to build a similar one near the Emerson home. For this labor Mr. Alcott received fifty dollars. The recompense, welcome as it was, weighed but as a trifle in comparison with the satisfaction Mr. Alcott felt in his creative artistry. Heart and soul he threw himself into its design and building.

Of all Mr. Alcott's friends, Mr. Emerson was the one with whom he was most intimate. Often Mr. Emerson's tall figure would be seen coming along the road to Hillside, and his gentle voice would be heard inquiring for Mr. Alcott. Then they would enjoy a long evening of conversation in the study. Mr. Alcott believed in the virtues of conversation with its opportunity for the rapid exchange of ideas. In his diary he usually mentioned the topic of discussion. Describing the evening of May 28, 1846, he wrote:

> We had some talk on *Behmen's Doctrine of Signatures* and on the *Law of Images and Sounds.* I said that when sound assumes figure, or approaches towards shape, one derives a high pleasure from it as in Epic song.

He had begun his entry with the following interesting comment:

> *Emerson* spent the evening with me; he showed me Carlyle's daguerreotype profile miniature which he has just received. I thought it very good—the same compression of lip and depth of eye, that I retain from memory of him.

What pleasure they must have had studying the picture by lamplight and reminiscing about their English friend!

On many Sundays Mr. Alcott spent part of the day "conversing" and walking with Mr. Emerson. Often they strolled in Walden Woods. One of their delightful Sunday observances was the gathering of their own children and also some of their neighbors' at the Emerson schoolroom. There would be a reading from the Bible or some other selection chosen by Mr. Alcott, followed by a brief discussion, in terms which the children could understand, of some subject of interest to them. In her diary Beth recorded such a Sunday in September, 1846:

> Father went with us to meeting at Mr. Emersons. Elizabeth Goodwin brought in to the school room, a little dead squirrel in a paper coffin, and this gave us something to talk about.

Her father, describing the same meeting, wrote in his diary:

Discoursed with the *Children at Emersons* on Respect for Human Life and Tenderness to the Inferior Animals. The Conversation descended to some of the causes which provoke ill-nature, and set creatures at variance. The doctrine of Diet was quite boldly elucidated—the children mainly inclined to take the side of clemency and elegancy against their own appetites.

Another of Mr. Alcott's friends, almost as intimate as Mr. Emerson, was Mr. Thoreau. He had built his hut at Walden Pond at about the time the Alcotts moved into Hillside. Often Mr. Alcott walked to the "Hermitage at Walden," as he once called it in his diary, and spent long hours with his friend, conversing or listening. He spent the afternoon and evening of December 31, 1846 there, while Mr. Thoreau read him many passages from his *Week on the Concord and Merrimac Rivers*. On other occasions Mr. Thoreau would walk across the meadows to Hillside; one afternoon he read the first part of his lecture on Diogenes's life to a group of Mrs. Alcott's friends. In the evening the group went to the Lyceum to hear him read the second part. Many happy hours were spent in the Hillside study by Mr. Thoreau and Mr. Alcott, who wrote in his diary on January 13, 1848:

> *Henry Thoreau* came in after my hours with the children, and we had a good deal of talk on the modes

of popular influence. He read me a *MS Essay of his on Friendship* which he has just written. . . .

Not content, however, always to remain indoors, they often took long walks together in their beloved woods.

Another friend, whom Mr. Alcott learned to know better during 1847 and 1848, was the poet, William Ellery Channing. A walk with this friend, doubtless typical of many walks with Mr. Emerson and Mr. Thoreau, is beautifully described by Mr. Alcott in his diary, dated February 1, 1848:

> *Walked to Walden with Channing.* He admired the clear serene blue of the Sky, which amidst the falling snow flakes, was almost as warm and hazy as the summer heavens. The Clouds piled above Wachuset in the west, were magnificent, and some lying in buried repose about its base, were worthy the pencil of Rhembrandt [*sic*]. Altogether our walk and conversation, especially on Goose Pond under the brow of the pine grove, was lively suggestive and memorable. We talked of Art, and the new Pantheon. We tried to name the Gods whom some Angelo or Raphael is to paint. C thinks *Pantheism* is the only religion now left for us and that the old *Zoroastrian rites become us,* in so fine a Nature as ours here in this new-World. The *worship of the Sun* at dawn and at setting would at least promote the circulation of the spirits

in which Piety, and the elements of a lively worship, consist.

Returning, we talked of the possibility of some
close union, if not of families, then meeting at a
Common Room in the village, whensoever we might
choose, for *conversation* and *reading*.

The gathering of a group for the discussion of
philosophical subjects, or of topics of a timely interest,
had long been dear to Mr. Alcott's heart. He had been
delighted when some of his townspeople had asked
him to meet with them regularly for such discussions.
On Thursday, April 9, 1846, he wrote in his diary of his
"circle for *Conversation*" which met that evening at
Mrs. Barlow's in the village, and to which Anna accompanied her father. Weekly meetings were held that spring
and fall. In March of the next year a group of Concord
men met at Hillside to consider the possibility of a
village club for discussion, but unfortunately the plan
was not carried out. When Mr. Alcott talked with Mr.
Channing, as described above, he was still hopeful. His
wish was finally fulfilled late in 1848, after he and his
family had left Hillside and had moved into Boston.

Alcott's desire for such meetings was stimulated by
a very keen interest in the social problems of the day,
especially in the anti-slavery movement and in peace
and other questions connected with the Mexican War.

He and his wife had for many years been warm friends of Theodore Parker, William Lloyd Garrison, and other farsighted men, and had kept in touch with their activities. Mr. Alcott described a meeting which was held in Boston, on May 28, 1847, at which twenty-six persons were present. Among them were such leading reformers as Mrs. Lucretia Mott, Garrison, Wendell Phillips, Parker, Charles Sumner, W. H. Channing, and Samuel J. May, as well as Mr. Emerson and Dr. Samuel Gridley Howe. Mr. Alcott wrote:

> Met at Parkers the following Persons and discussed during the afternoon and evening, some of the great questions of the time—our main topic for conversation—*the aspects and methods of Reform* . . . The conversation was lively, unusually fine, and passages profoundly eloquent; this meeting, while greater numbers were brought together, and of a wider variety of sentiment, than in our former circles, was characterized by an uncommon courtesy, and depth of sentiment. There was the eloquence of character to dignify our convention. It was *a setting of the times* . . .

After further comments about the meeting, he wrote of his pleasure at being able to speak to such a group since it offered an opportunity "to move the living times, as they were its head and teachers."

Both Mr. and Mrs. Alcott had long been interested in social problems. They had been prominent members of the community at Fruitlands, in Harvard, Massachusetts, which was organized by Alcott in company with the English mystic, Charles Lane. It was but one of the numerous co-operative communities devoted to plain living and high thinking which appeared in America during this period. The experiment, which lasted from June, 1843 to January, 1844, had left the Alcotts financially and physically exhausted. Although it failed, they were still keenly interested in the betterment of mankind.

Among the guests who were welcomed to Hillside during the first year of the Alcotts' residence there was Charles Lane, who had provided much of the money for the experiment at Fruitlands. After its collapse he and his son William, who had accompanied him to the United States, lived for a time with the Shakers. When the Alcotts had become fairly well settled at Hillside, Mr. Lane came to stay with them. Since he was soon to return to England, he brought his books to Hillside, and asked Mr. Alcott to take charge of them. Mrs. Alcott wrote of the meeting of the two friends: "The reunion between him and Mr. Alcott was quite affecting—for it was so unlooked for by the latter."

As it turned out, Mr. Lane's visit came at an opportune time for the Alcotts. Mr. Alcott, who was suddenly called to the sickbed of his brother Junius, needed someone to whom he could entrust the teaching of his children and the tending of his vegetables. Although Mr. Alcott was away only a week, Mr. Lane remained at Hillside for two months that summer and fall, and again for a short time the following year before his return to England.

When the British social reformer, Robert Owen, visited Hillside in the fall of 1845, the Alcotts listened eagerly while he told them of his hopes for socialized living. Mrs. Alcott wrote to her brother, Samuel J. May, that Owen "detailed minutely his scheme at New Lancaster—also at New Harmony." Her letter shows how much in sympathy she was with Owen's plans for a proposed new world order, and how heartily she agreed with his estimate of the five great evils from which he believed society was suffering. She wrote:

> Mr. Owen is the most hopeful person I have ever met—feeling quite sure that he shall see a radical change while he lives. I admire his enthusiasm.

Since Concord wished to meet the distinguished visitor, Mrs. Alcott, ever hospitably inclined, rose to the occasion:

> We got up a large party for him and by 8 ock our rooms were filled—much to his satisfaction and the delight of the company. Though unfeasted and unpledged—our guests left us feeling that the true hospitality was love and intelligence—

To an unusual extent Mrs. Alcott shared the varied interests of her husband. Both came from intellectual families. To both of them, even in childhood, books, especially the classics, had been part of their daily living. Both were firm abolitionists. Mr. Alcott indeed once took his life in his hands when, deserted by his friends, he mounted a flight of stairs in an attempt to rescue a runaway slave from his captors. Mrs. Alcott's realization of the need for social reform was fully as keen as her husband's. She was a member of a family with strong humanitarian interests. In her correspondence with her brother, Samuel J. May, a noted abolitionist, she made frequent sympathetic comments upon the progress of the movement and discussed the abilities of its leaders.

Early in 1847 the Alcotts themselves gave protection to an escaped slave. Mrs. Alcott wrote to her brother on January 13, describing this experience:

We have had an interesting fugitive here for 2 weeks—right from Maryland. He was anxious to get to Canada and we have forwarded him the best way we could. His sufferings have been great, his intrepidity unparalleled. He agrees with us about Slave produce—he says it is the only way the Abolition of the Slave can ever be effected. He says it will never be done by insurrection . . .

Mr. Alcott wrote in his diary, describing the fugitive:

> He is scarce thirty years of age, athletic, dextrous, sagacious, and self-relying, he has many of the elements of a hero. His stay with us has given image and a name to the dire entity of Slavery, and was an impressive lesson to my children, bringing before them the wrongs of the Black man, and his tale of woes.

The fugitive cut and stacked wood for Mr. Alcott on the Hillside terraces, but it is probable that a hiding place had been prepared against a sudden search by the sheriff. They may have utilized the space near the chimney of the southeast bedroom.

The anti-slavery movement was a very real link between the Alcotts and their friends in Boston. When he could no longer endure the drudgery of his farming, Mr. Alcott would go to Boston, see his anti-slavery friends, attend their private as well as public meetings, and come back with renewed courage to undertake again his manual toil. Occasionally he went to other cities. In November, 1846, he visited friends in Providence and made addresses before the Abolition Society, the Teachers' Institute, and the Peace Society. Mrs. Alcott also felt the stimulus of trips to Boston. Her relatives and friends were prominent in progressive movements, and she had a wide and distinguished circle of acquaintances.

In their homes she was in touch once more with what was taking place in the world. On returning to Concord, she found her mind filled with memories of good talks and of the meetings she had attended.

After such visits to Boston Mrs. Alcott's letters to her brother and his family or to friends show how wholeheartedly she had entered into their life, how courageous and discerning was her own spirit and mind, and how intuitively quick she was to share joy or sorrow. Both she and her husband cherished the ties of friendship and of kinship and welcomed every opportunity for greater association. Her invitations to friends and relatives were cordial and sincere. Many times, and affectionately, she urged her husband's aged mother to make her home with them.

The frugal way of living which the Alcotts had practiced at Fruitlands was continued at Hillside, but with less severity. They did not, however, eat meat or other animal products, although Mrs. Alcott and the girls had milk and cheese. In addition they avoided, as far as possible, the use of articles produced by slave labor, believing that such abstinence, if practiced by all persons, would quickly force slaveholders to free their slaves. Mr. Alcott mentioned with regret in his diary, on May 11, 1846, that they were unable to do without cotton and leather since one involved the sacrifice of Negroes, and the other of animals. This attitude towards defenseless creatures sprang not only from the Alcotts' natural kindness of heart, but also from their belief that life was under the direct guidance of a Divine Providence and that it was man's duty to resist all forms of cruelty, intolerance, and strife, and to keep himself in harmony with spiritual forces. Daily living, they believed, should be conducted with gentleness as well as with vigor.

Filled as was Mr. Alcott's mind with humanitarian and educational reforms, and interested as he was in philosophy, it is not strange that he spent long hours reading and writing during the winter months, or at other times when he could not farm. The number of the books he read, and their quality, show his love of literature, his scholarly mind, and the wide range of his interests. His was indeed no casual reading: pages of his diaries, especially for Sunday when he did no manual work, are filled with quotations from books he had borrowed, critical analyses of what he had read, or with discussions of an author's theories, literary accomplishments, or character. Often these comments were followed by his own philosophical beliefs, and his reactions to recent events, or to some beauty of nature which had stirred him. His fondness for poetry is evidenced by his quotations from it, and by his own verse.

It was unfortunate that the Alcotts, with their scholarly interests and humanitarian ideals, did not have enough money to live comfortably in the home which they had worked so hard to beautify. Even when they were making their first arrangements, Mr. Alcott had tried to plan economically. He had asked his brother Junius to share the place with them, partly because he longed for his companionship, and partly because he thought that Junius could earn money by his cabinet work, as well as help in the farm work. When his brother was unable to come, Mr. Alcott had attempted to establish a small school in Concord. Although he engaged the services of an excellent assistant, a Miss Sophia Ford, formerly of Northampton, the project did not materialize. On its failure he turned with what courage and philosophic gratitude he could muster, as we have seen, to the raising of vegetables and other farm produce. All that his family did not need he sold to his neighbors, or exchanged for their services in plowing or other especially heavy work, such as digging the ditches for the Garden House, and building stone walls.

Mrs. Alcott aided him in every way possible, even admitting to their household children who needed, for one reason or another, to be boarded in the country in a family. Although the resulting money payments were gladly received, her attitude towards these children was one of motherly interest and self-sacrifice. With regard to one little boarder who needed particular care, she wrote, "I shall have less time for reading and other pursuits with my girls; but if by faithful care of this bewildered child we can make her path more sunny and straight I shall be well repaid for the sacrifice of personal comfort."

One orphan boy who spent some of his summer vacations with the Alcotts at Hillside, in later years wrote a loving description of the happy family life he shared with them in the old house.

. . . Mrs. Alcott was sunshine itself to her children and to me, whom she looked upon as a son. No matter how weary she might be with the washing and ironing, the baking and cleaning, it was all hidden from the group of girls with whom she was always ready to enter into fun and frolic, as though she never had a care. Afternoons we usually gathered in the quaint, simple, charming, old-fashioned parlor at Hillside . . . To this day, over all the years, that simple Concord room with its pretty chintz curtains, its cool matting, its few fine engravings . . . its books and cut flowers, and its indescribable atmosphere of refinement, is deeply engraved within my memory as an expression of inherent simplicity and charm.

One of our number, usually myself, would read aloud while the mother and the two elder daughters engaged in the family sewing. Thus we read Scott, Dickens, Cooper, Hawthorne, Shakespeare and the British poets, and George Sand's "Consuelo." Mrs.

Alcott's comments upon and explanations of our reading, when we questioned, were most instructive to us in beauty of expression, and revealed the wealth of her own richly stored mind. Mr. Alcott's table talks were constantly delightful. It was particularly at these times he took especial care to so discourse that the youngest listener might comprehend and fully understand. I have seen him take an apple upon his fork, and while preparing it for eating, give a fascinating little lecture as to its growth and development from germ to matured fruit, his language quaintly beautiful and charmingly poetical.

A child in speaking of him in my hearing said: "I love to hear him talk. He is so plain and tells me so much I didn't know, fastening it on to what I know."

He rarely talked of else at table but nature's wonderful and benevolent processes in preparing food for the maintenance of man and in ministering to his taste through her countless presentations of the beautiful. Indeed his great love of nature, his keen, close observation of all her processes and his power of expression, all combined to make him charmingly instructive and entertaining.[5]

---

[5] Quoted from *Alcott Memoirs*, Posthumously Compiled from Papers, Journals, and Memoranda of the late Dr. Frederick L. H. Willis, by E. W. L. and H. B. (1915), pp. 24–26.

In spite of the best efforts of Mr. and Mrs. Alcott, there was need of more money than they could provide while they remained in Concord. In addition the girls were growing into young womanhood, and were ready for wider educational advantages. Anna had kept at her studies, had received German lessons from Mr. George Bradford, and had helped to teach her younger sisters and the Emerson children, after their teacher, Miss Ford, had left for the summer. In the fall of 1847 Anna was given the opportunity to teach a small school at Walpole, New Hampshire, and to live with a dear friend of Mrs. Alcott's. Since Anna remained at Walpole during the summer of 1848, Louisa, at the request of Mrs. Emerson, undertook the task of teaching the Emerson children, holding her classes in the Hillside barn. At about this time Louisa told Ellen Emerson a number of fairy tales, later putting them into written form and sending them to her little friend. Several years later these little stories appeared in print, Louisa's first book, *Flower Fables*.

During 1847 and 1848 there had been talk of selling Hillside and of moving into Boston where Mr. Alcott might earn money by giving "Conversations" to groups of the literati, and where teaching opportunities and educational advantages were accessible for the girls. Late in the fall of 1848 a social-service position was secured for Mrs. Alcott, and on November 17 the Alcotts moved into Boston, for their new venture.

Under Hawthorne's
Many Roofs

UNA   ROSE

NATHANIEL HAWTHORNE

JULIAN   MRS. HAWTHORNE

The day of plain living and high thinking at Hillside had not ended with the departure of the Alcott family. In 1852 Nathaniel Hawthorne and his family took up their residence in the old house. Hawthorne was interested in discovering those psychological processes which determine men's actions and mold their lives, realizing that only through such knowledge could he faithfully portray in his books the realities of life. Although he often took a hidden misdeed as the motivating incident, his interest was not in sin as such, but in the effect of any important and disturbing event upon the future life of the individual concerned. His ability to understand human nature and to portray it in living words is so well known that it needs no discussion in a brief description of his home life. His eminence as an author has, however, too often overshadowed his eminence as a man, lovable, humorous, upright, and practical in the world of politics and of men.

To Mr. Hawthorne, as to Mr. Alcott, came the desire to own a home. By 1852 he was financially able to fulfill this desire, his literary fame having been established with the publication of *The Scarlet Letter* and *The House of the Seven Gables*. He was nearly forty-eight years of age, a strong, well-built, handsome man, whose grace and endurance in skating are well known. His erect carriage, his penetrating eyes, and a lurking smile made him look younger than his years, and expressed the vigor of his mind and the underlying wit and humor. These qualities of mind and body are particularly noticeable in the portrait which George P. A. Healey painted soon after Mr. Hawthorne's arrival at The Wayside.

Mrs. Hawthorne, an attractive woman five years his junior, was well equipped mentally and spiritually to be a real helpmate to her husband. She was devoted to him, aiding him in conquering his shyness, yet standing as an unyielding bulwark against anyone intruding upon his privacy. They were so close in spirit that she understood his moods; her love made her long to smooth life's path for him.

Una, with the sunny hair, was eight years of age, the eldest of three children. Elf-like, merry and sad by turns, she was an enigma and a challenge to her father. His long and charming description of her, which has fortunately for us been preserved by Col. Thomas Wentworth Higginson in *Part of a Man's Life,* gives a keen analysis of her conflicting moods and traits when a will-of-the-wisp child of seven. Julian, the only son, was to be six years old on June 22. He was an active child who developed a passion for turtles, the brook, and other outdoor enticements. Baby Rose, appropriately nicknamed Rosebud, was a jolly, pink-cheeked, blue-eyed toddler, with the same red-gold hair that her sister possessed. Just a year old, she was everywhere and into everything, yet demurely followed her mother and Mrs. Emerson around when the latter, with her sister, came to call.

Like the Alcotts before them, the Hawthornes had been living in rented quarters, none too happily. For the year 1850-1851 they had leased a little red cottage in Lenox, but certain unpleasant conditions there had made them determine to move. While looking around for a permanent home, they were able to rent for the winter the West Newton house of Mrs. Hawthorne's brother-in-law, Horace Mann. Since he and his family would return from Washington when Congress adjourned, it was necessary for the Hawthornes to make other arrangements in the spring. Although Mr. Hawthorne loved the sea, and would have liked to settle near it, his mind must have been turned towards Concord by the friendships and happy memories of the three years which he and his wife had spent in the quiet village. Nine years earlier, at the time of his marriage in 1842, he had rented the Old Manse, and to it had brought his bride. There his eldest child, Una, had been born. Thus he and his wife were disposed to consider the Alcott house when mutual friends suggested it.

The sale was completed in March, 1852, but the Hawthorne family did not move into their new home until the first week in June. Mrs. Hawthorne, Una, and the baby Rose preceded Mr. Hawthorne and Julian by a few days. Thus Mrs. Hawthorne was able to make preliminary repairs, and to arrange the furniture and carpets so that her husband had a "civilized impression" of their new home, as she remarked in a chatty letter to her mother. Always keenly appreciative of beautiful things, she was pleased with the new carpet for the study; it looked like rich velvet, a ground work of lapis-lazuli blue, upon which was an acanthus pattern of fine wood color, with an occasional rose and green leaf. The dining room had a handsome paper with a silvery sheen; on the floor was a brown and green Brussels carpet. The wood-work of the lower rooms was painted to resemble oak.

When Mr. Hawthorne and Julian drove up in the carriage on Saturday, June 5, there was a joyful reunion of a happy family, delighted that at last they owned a house of their own. In a letter written ten days after his arrival, Mr. Hawthorne asked his friend, Mr. Evert Duyckinck, Editor of the *Literary World,* to send the magazine to "Concord (Mass) where I have bought a house, and feel myself, for the first time in my life, at home." Mr. Hawthorne added:

> Alcott called it "Hillside" as it stands close at the base of a steep ascent; but as it also [is] in proximity (too nigh, indeed) to the road leading into the village, I have rebaptized it "The Wayside"—which seems to me to possess a moral as well as a descriptive propriety. It might have been called "Wood-side"—the hill being covered with a growth of birch, locust-trees, and various sorts of pine.

Many of Mr. Alcott's trees, particularly the pines in front of the house, had survived, and gave not only pleasant shade but also some protection from the road dust, as he had hoped when he planted them.

Like many new home owners, the Hawthornes arranged for the replanting of the garden which had been neglected by tenants after the Alcotts had moved into Boston. In a letter to her mother, Mrs. Hawthorne wrote that her husband cut his bean poles on his own land. It was a delightful sensation to be a home owner, and to be freed, at least temporarily, from the fatigue of writing, however pleasant an occupation it ordinarily might be. He had very recently finished *The Blithedale*

The Wayside in 1853.   After an Old Drawing

Romance, and was ready to enjoy a well-won relaxation. In the letter to Mr. Duyckinck he wrote:

> I see that the papers announce me as having begun a new work, the day after finishing the Blithedale Romance. My poor intellect is not quite so ready and flexible as that. It is now six weeks since I finished the romance; and I have neither written nor thought of the first sentence of another book.

He was not destined, however, to be long free from literary work, nor, when he did start to write, was he free to take up what he had happily planned, another book for children, to follow *A Wonder Book.* Almost on the day of his arrival at The Wayside, his good friend and Bowdoin classmate, Franklin Pierce, was nominated for the Presidency of the United States. Mr. Hawthorne realized that his friend might well turn to him for the necessary campaign biography. Such a task would be particularly distasteful to him; he was looking forward contentedly to writing this book for children; he did not want to write a biography; least of all did he want to appear to be buying a political appointment. He was aware that his friend, if elected, would probably give him a lucrative post, and a biography at that time might seem to the public like a purchase price. In order to forestall such a request, he wrote immediately, suggesting that Mr. Pierce secure the services of Mr. Charles C.

Hazewell of Concord, who was connected with the *Boston Daily Times,* and was a ready and effective speaker with extensive information on political and other subjects. He offered, however, to help Mr. Hazewell in any way he could.

Mr. Hawthorne's efforts to avoid the embarrassing task were doomed to failure. Within a week, after a personal interview in which he again stressed his own inadequacy, he had consented to write the book. His sense of loyalty to a friend, a marked characteristic of Mr. Hawthorne, had overcome his better judgment. He wrote to Horatio Bridge, a mutual friend of Bowdoin College days: "Of course, after a friendship of thirty years, it was impossible to refuse my best efforts in his behalf at this—the great pinch of his life." [1] Then began a two and a half months' rush to secure accurate information. Mr. Hawthorne's intellectual honesty would not allow him to write anything but the truth; yet his insight into human nature made him realize that General Pierce must be made a popular figure in order to be elected,—a statesman as well as a gallant soldier. In a long letter to the general under date of July 5, he wrote:

I am sensible of a very difficult and delicate part of my task, in your connection with the great subject of

---

[1] Horatio Bridge, *Personal Recollections of Nathaniel Hawthorne* (Harper & Brothers, 1893), p. 131.

variance between the North and the South. There is no way, however, open to my perception—no course either of true policy, or worthy either of you or your biographer—save to meet the question with perfect candor and frankness, and to state what has been your action, and what your position; not pugnaciously, and, by no manner of means, defensively, but so as to put you on the broadest ground possible, as a man for the whole country.

The summer of 1852, therefore, was filled with interviews at The Wayside and elsewhere, with the writing of letters of inquiry, and finally with the irksome task of rapid composition. Speed, such as was necessary for a campaign biography, was not customary for Mr. Hawthorne, who usually consumed much time pacing back and forth, carefully planning his sentences before committing them to paper. By the end of August the biography was finished, except for the reading of proof, and Mr. Hawthorne was free to attend his class reunion at Bowdoin College and later to go to the Isles of Shoals for a rest beside his much-loved sea.

A vacation at this time was almost imperative for Mr. Hawthorne. During the summer of 1852, while he was in the midst of his uncongenial task, he received word of the tragic death of his younger sister Louisa, who was drowned at the time of the burning of the steamer, *Henry Clay*. She was traveling by that boat from Albany to New York, on her way to The Wayside, where she had expected to make a long visit. She and her brother had been close in spirit from childhood days, and her sudden death was a severe blow to him. Years later Julian writes that his father listened to the news without a word, then walked to the hill, and "was seen no more that day."

During Mr. Hawthorne's absence at Bowdoin College and on the Isles of Shoals his wife kept a full account of the activities of the little household, so that on his return he might feel that he had not missed any of the happy family life. She began her diary thus:

Concord, Mass. 1852
August 30th, Monday.

This morning at $\frac{1}{2}$ past 8 my husband went to Boston on his way to Brunswick to attend the Commencement of his Alma Mater. It was & is a sullen cold rainstorm, & at this moment (9 o'clk evening) seems no nearer fair weather than when the light of all our seeing went away. Una was very pensive for a great while—but soon she & Julian began to wonder how it would seem to Papa when he got back if they should never tease one another, never frown nor fret, always mind when spoken to—if Papa should hear only lovely tones & see only pleasant faces—and all this joined to baby's angel talk & angel smiles, thought Una, would make Papa think he was in heaven with us—"Or," said Julian, "not with *us* but with some other children"—"Yes," I replied, "with your spirits." "Oh," they both exclaimed, "let us try & try & try & *perhaps* we can!" & both faces looked like both a prayer & a hope & also a thanksgiving. Baby attended to their conversation & observed their expressions & made a sage remark upon the subject which caused a general shout of "Oh angel!" & seemed to settle the whole matter.

They really were good children; Mrs. Hawthorne often mentions that early in the morning, or when she was resting, Una would of her own accord keep her six-year-old brother quiet by reading aloud to him. On one occasion Mrs. Hawthorne wrote, "Una & Julian have been very good. They feel a responsibility about me which is beautiful to see." Yet they were not always angelic; Una, in her elfish mischief, once threw burrs into Julian's long curls. They were like all children. "Two thirds celestial," Mrs. Hawthorne once described Una.

They were a happy group. Mrs. Hawthorne wrote one evening, describing the antics of the children:

We had a very merry time after tea, for Una undertook to be comical, & to imitate characters

—& she was irresistible. We nearly died of laughing & Julian exploded in a way that was alarming to hear! It certainly never will do for him to be with people who act as funny as they can. Baby joined in & laughed for sympathy. The fun & the laughing took so much time that it was eight before Una got to bed.

Their family life, however, was not complete without their father. Of Rose, who was just beginning to talk, her mother wrote:

Baby has talked a great deal about Papa today, & at tea time turned around of her own thought to his portrait & held a long & elaborate discourse about it, pointing to it all the time. I only wish I could have understood her idiom. She was sitting with me in the study when she heard Julian's voice talking with Una on his return from the village, & she shouted Dère Papa—dère Papa—dère Papa & stretched out to see him with the most joyful smile.

The older children were equally devoted to their father. One day as Julian was talking with his mother about growing older, he turned to her and said, "Will papa be as beautiful as now when he grows older? . . . There cannot be so good & beautiful an angel in Heaven." In speaking of the children's impatience for their father's return, Mrs. Hawthorne wrote: "Julian wants to know if I expect him this morning, this afternoon, to-morrow—tonight—& every other assignable hour." On another day she noted, "Never was father, never was husband so loved & longed for." Una, many years later, said of her father that he was one of the gayest persons she had ever known, and the best playmate anyone could ask for.

When Mr. Hawthorne returned, in the middle of September, browned and refreshed by his vacation at the sea, there were many happy times for the family. They enjoyed picking their good peaches and Porter apples from their own trees, the same trees which Mr. Alcott had hopefully planted on the terraces. Mrs. Hawthorne has written of Sunday afternoons spent on these terraces, her husband stretched out beside her, as they listened to the wind in the trees, or the sound of the children at play. Sometimes they all sat on the top of the hill, and made gaily colored wreaths from the red and gold leaves. At other times the parents watched the children working in their gardens on the terraces. "They intend to lay out their farms in *beds,* Una said," Mrs. Hawthorne once wrote, and added:

> They looked so pretty up on the terraces at work in the golden light. What a charming place this is for them & for all of us.

They did love their new estate. Mr. Hawthorne, in a letter to a friend, describing the wooded hillside, and the shade to be found on it, wrote:

> I spend delectable hours there in the hottest part of the day, stretched out at my lazy length, with a book in my hand or an unwritten book in my thoughts. There is almost always a breeze stirring along the side or brow of the hill.[2]

The Hawthornes, however, did not live to themselves alone. There were many visits back and forth with their Concord friends. The Emersons were particularly kind and included the Hawthorne children in picnics and other festivities. Julian, much to his joy, was taught to ride Edward Emerson's pony, a living one this time, and not the wooden horse on which so many Emerson children had played in their younger years, and which other generations of Concord children have since that time enjoyed.

On the other side of The Wayside lived Mr. Ephraim Wales Bull and his small family. He had originally been a goldbeater, as has been mentioned, and had come to Concord in 1836 to spend the last six months which his doctor had given him to live. He had turned horticulturist, and raised beautiful roses, peaches, grapes, and other fruits and flowers, ulti-

---

[2] George Parsons Lathrop, *A Study of Hawthorne* (1876), pp. 243–244.

mately originating the Concord grape. His little daughter, Mary Ellen, was a member of the Sunday-school
class which Mrs. Hawthorne conducted for her own
children and those of a few neighbors. The two families
were friendly and many gifts from Mr. Bull's garden
found their way to The Wayside. He was always generous with his lovely old-fashioned roses, and he took
delight in opening his greenhouses to various generations
of neighborhood children.

When I knew Mr. Bull, he was old and grayhaired.
During the time that the Hawthornes lived at The
Wayside, however, he was very active and took part in
Concord town affairs, holding various offices, among
them that of selectman. He was a welcome visitor at
The Wayside, Mr. Hawthorne enjoying the honesty of
speech and the clear brain of his neighbor. They often
sat in Mr. Alcott's old summerhouse on the terraces,
and discussed politics and human nature.

That same summerhouse Mr. Hawthorne described
when he finally became free to turn to his new book for
children, *Tanglewood Tales*. In the introductory section,
which he entitled "The Wayside," he wrote of the arbor:

> It is a mere skeleton of slender, decaying tree
> trunks, with neither walls nor a roof; nothing but a
> tracery of branches and twigs, which the next wintry
> blast will be very likely to scatter in fragments along

the terrace. It looks, and is, as evanescent as a dream; and yet, in its rustic network of boughs, it has somehow enclosed a hint of spiritual beauty, and has become a true emblem of the subtile and ethereal mind that planned it . . . Simple as it looks . . . this little edifice seems to be the work of magic. It is full of suggestiveness, and, in its way, is as good as a cathedral. Ah, it would be just the spot for one to sit in, of a summer afternoon, and tell the children some more of those wild stories from the classic myths!

To the adaptation of these myths, which he had put aside for the unwelcome task of the Pierce biography, he turned with pleasure. He enjoyed children and was particularly happy when writing for them. His cheerfulness with young people was remarked by Mr. Moncure D. Conway, who observed that Mr. Hawthorne was almost merry at a children's party at the Conway house and especially enjoyed a charade on the word "transcendentalism." On another occasion, a children's picnic in the woods near Walden Pond, Mr. Hawthorne persuaded Mrs. Conway to hide him in a thicket, so that he might watch the children while they played and danced without the restraint his presence might have caused. When he was working on the myths, he read aloud each evening to Una and to Julian what he had written that day, and listened to their criticisms. A pretty family group it must have been, the two eager and attractive children listening to their handsome father as they sat in front of the soapstone stove in the sitting room, or in the little study which had been Mr. Alcott's. The companionship with his children in the work of adapting these myths was a happy contrast to the irksome demands which politics were even then making upon his time and attention.

Immediately after the election of General Pierce, all sorts and conditions of men appealed to Mr. Hawthorne, by letter and in person, for advice or other assistance in political preferment. To each he conscientiously gave a hearing, although he commented to a friend that he wished that he might go to Boston "incognito" since he was "beset" by so many importunities. For most of these applicants he wrote letters and did what he could. For his friends he exerted every pressure possible, albeit with a discerning, if kindly, realization of their handicaps. A striking example of his loyalty is his almost impassioned appeal to William B. Pike of Salem, in behalf of their friend, "Zack" Burchmore; yet even in this appeal he recognized Mr. Burchmore's weaknesses. Mr. Hawthorne's was a practical mind; he knew men, politicians particularly, after his experiences at the Boston and the Salem customhouses, and his appeals, as well as his advice, were tinged with a realistic humor.

Randall Stewart has pointed out in his article, "Hawthorne and Politics," that "The study of Hawthorne's political career reveals with special illumination certain distinctive aspects of his personality: his democracy, his loyalty to friends, his practicality, his shrewdness, his skill in diplomacy, and his remarkable sense of humor."[3]

On March 26, 1853, the appointment of Mr. Hawthorne to the Consulship at Liverpool had been confirmed by the Senate, as the cheery note written by Mr. Charles Sumner testifies:

> "Good! good!" I exclaimed aloud on the floor of the Senate as your nomination was announced.
>
> "Good! good!" I now write to you, on its confirmation. Nothing could be more grateful to me. Before you go, I hope to see you.[4]

The enthusiasm of this note was echoed by the many friends of Mr. Hawthorne, who considered that this appointment honored all concerned. Early in April, even before the proofs of *Tanglewood Tales* were all in his hands, Mr. Hawthorne traveled to Washington with his good friend Mr. William D. Ticknor, the senior partner of his publishing firm. Although Mr. Hawthorne's pri-

---

[3] "Hawthorne and Politics: Unpublished Letters to William B. Pike," edited by Randall Stewart, *The New England Quarterly*, V, 243 (April, 1932).

[4] Lathrop, *op. cit.*, p. 248.

mary purpose in making the trip was to confer with the President and other officials in preparation for his future duties in England, nevertheless he did not overlook an opportunity to help a friend. In his letter of April 6, he wrote, not disclosing, however, the friend's identity:

> Dear Ticknor,
>
> I think we had better be off as soon as the book is in type—which I suppose it will be in the course of next week. In fact, I should not object to going early in the week, whether or no. A friend, to whom I am indebted for many kindnesses, thinks that I might be of service to him there; and I should at least like to try.

At the conclusion of the trip he wrote that he had enjoyed a visit to Mt. Vernon with the President's family in delightful spring weather, and was glad that during his stay in Washington he had accomplished much, both for others and for himself. Agreeable as was his visit, he missed his family and rejoiced when he could turn homeward.

There were many preparations to be made for the long absence abroad: letters to be burned; arrangements to be completed with Mrs. Hawthorne's brother, Dr. Nathaniel Peabody, who was to occupy and care for the house; and farewell dinners to attend. Mr. Longfellow gave an especially happy one, and wrote in his diary the next day, "The memory of yesterday sweetens today." He added that he was glad his old friend had seemed lively and in good spirits. The friendship between the two men, although undemonstrative, was a deep and abiding one. Shortly before sailing, Mr. Hawthorne wrote to break an engagement with Mr. Longfellow, whom he had wanted to see, even if only for a moment in the midst of the busy preparations for departure. He added that he hoped that Mr. Longfellow regretted his breaking the appointment half as much as he himself regretted it.

To the Hawthornes, who expected to remain abroad for at least five years, the parting from relatives and friends was not easy. Mrs. Hawthorne had dreaded to leave her invalid mother, but had been spared that particular distress by the sufferer's death during the preceding winter. The emotions of the Hawthorne family were mixed as they sailed from home: to the children the departure was all joy and adventure; to their parents it meant separation from loved ones, the challenge of an unknown and official environment, but still an opportunity to visit historic spots and a meeting with literary friends who had long been urging Mr. Hawthorne to visit England.

Seven years passed before the Hawthornes finally returned to their home. The visit to Italy prolonged their stay until 1859; Una's serious illness in Rome delayed them another year. When they learned from her doctor that she was too weak to undertake a long sea trip, they found that Dr. Peabody had already made arrangements for a new home. As he could not readjust his plans, The Wayside was left vacant for a short time.

In the same summer occurred the sudden death of Horace Mann, the noted educator. His wife, Mary Peabody Mann, was a sister of Mrs. Hawthorne. When the news of her great loss reached the Hawthornes, they at once offered The Wayside to her and her three sons, for the period before their own return.

While Mrs. Mann was occupying The Wayside, the old house was again involved, although on this occasion more slightly, in alarms which preceded war. In April, 1860, an attempt had been made by officers representing the United States Senate to seize and take to Washington the Concord school teacher, Mr. Frank B. Sanborn. He was an intimate friend of the abolitionist John Brown and at the time was serving as his New England agent, although that relationship was not generally known. The government suspected, correctly, that Mr. Sanborn had important information and much correspondence from those interested in John Brown's plans. Although the first attempt to seize Mr. Sanborn was unsuccessful, his friends feared that he would ultimately be captured. For a week before they could make arrangements for his escape to Canada, he was hidden in seven different Concord houses, one of those nights being spent at The Wayside. Mr. Hawthorne has written that his sister-in-law, Mrs. Mann, contrived a hiding place in the garret. It is possible that she may have discovered the space near the chimney of the east bedroom, and gained access to it by removing attic floor boards.

When the Hawthornes returned to The Wayside, June 28, 1860, they found new neighbors, the Alcotts, occupying the dark brown house next door to The Wayside on the way to the village. These old friends of theirs had returned to Concord in 1857, in search of a new home. When they first arrived, they had for a week boarded with Dr. Peabody and his family, then living at The Wayside. Beth, particularly, had rejoiced to be able to return to the old house where she had spent happy years in her childhood. As soon as more perma-nent arrangements could be made, the family had moved to a house behind the Town Hall in the center of Con-cord. Beth was very frail, her weakness having come as a result of a serious attack of scarlet fever. She did not regain her strength, but steadily failed, and died in March, 1858. In the meantime the old house next to The Wayside had been purchased and was being remod-eled by Mr. Alcott. On April 1, 1858, his family again returned to the western wing of The Wayside to stay until their new home was ready. Mr. Alcott mentioned happily in his diary three days later that he was sitting

in Mr. Hawthorne's study, which had once been his
own study, the room where he had held long conversations with Mr. Emerson, Mr. Thoreau, and Mr.
Channing. In the summer of 1858 the Alcotts moved
into their new home, which they named Orchard House.
Under its elms Anna Alcott was married in 1860 to a
young Concord man, John Pratt, and with him moved
to Chelsea where he could be near his business. When
the Hawthornes returned to Concord, therefore, they
found only two of the Alcott daughters at Orchard
House.

To the Hawthornes the seven years abroad had
brought many changes, not only in the physical and
mental growth of the children, but in the social ease and
broadened experience of Mr. Hawthorne. With the
happiness there had come illness and worry. The climate
of England had proved harmful to Mrs. Hawthorne;
Una and Mr. Hawthorne had both been ill in Italy,
Una's illness nearly proving fatal. During his consulship
at Liverpool, Mr. Hawthorne had not been able to
undertake any writing, and it was not until after his
appointment was ended that he produced *The Marble
Faun*, begun in Italy, rewritten and completed in England.

On their return to Concord their friends welcomed
them joyfully. Mr. Emerson promptly invited a group
of Concord men to meet Mr. Hawthorne and to eat

strawberries and cream. Mr. Hawthorne, bronzed by the sea trip, surprised and pleased his townsmen by his increased ease of manner. In Boston, the publishing firm, Ticknor and Fields, gave a welcoming dinner.

The very evening of their arrival in Concord, on June 28, Mr. and Mrs. Alcott called upon them. In his diary, Mr. Alcott noted that the Hawthornes were well, and that Mr. Hawthorne was already talking about repairs and additions to the house, and was asking for suggestions about improving the grounds.

During the first few days at home, Mr. Hawthorne and Mr. Alcott walked around the estate and had a number of talks about needed alterations at The Wayside. At last Mr. Alcott took the carpenter, Mr. Wetherbee, to see Mr. Hawthorne, noting in his diary that Mr. Wetherbee "thinks the three story addition running up behind the present buildings the best, and will give H. an estimate of the cost and a drawing." The plan for this three-story addition was finally accepted, the room on the ground floor to be Mrs. Hawthorne's parlor, that on the second story to be the guest room, and Mr. Hawthorne's tower study to be on the top, where he could enjoy a wide view over the meadows of which he speaks affectionately in *Tanglewood Tales*. Mr. Hawthorne remembered with pleasure a half-ruined tower attached to Montauto, the castle which they had rented near Florence, Italy. Although its bats and ill-repair had

prevented him from using it as much as he would
have liked, its privacy had appealed to him. He must
have remembered, too, the beautiful sunsets which he
and his family had enjoyed as they looked from its top
over the Italian plains spread out below them. Now that

Tower Study Showing Hawthorne's Standing Desk

he was adding to his home, he determined to have a convenient place where he could watch the Concord sunsets, and, more important, where he could comfortably write, better protected from interruptions than he had been downstairs. The need of a new study was the more imperative because the changes proposed by the carpenter included moving the front door of the house to the western wing and placing it immediately next to the room in which Mr. Hawthorne had formerly worked.

Further additions to the house included an airy and sunny bedroom for Una, built over Mr. Hawthorne's previous study. Over the old kitchen was constructed a large room with an arched ceiling, devised, as her son states, to please Mrs. Hawthorne. Later this large room was divided into two small rooms for the maids. It is not strange that all these additions made necessary a new entrance and hall which would lead directly to the parlor on the ground floor of the three-story addition. In place of the old front door that had opened into the entry, dividing the rooms of the colonial house, a bay window was built. The entry thus became a pleasant little room into which the sun streamed all day long. In her letters Mrs. Hawthorne later spoke affectionately of it as "the chapel."

Changes were not confined to structural additions to the house. During the summer and early fall Mr. Alcott had been busy laying out paths for Mr. Hawthorne, making a rustic seat, and consulting with Mrs. Hawthorne about details of the work within the house.

Mrs. Hawthorne's artistic ability had early been shown in her illustrations of her husband's story, *The Gentle Boy*. She had already decorated their bedroom furniture with copies of Thorwaldson's and Flaxman's drawings. With the new additions to the house her artistic instinct came to the fore. The wallpaper chosen for her parlor was a lovely grayish shade stamped with a distinctive gold design. Most of the woodwork was "grained" in the style popular at that day. The paper of the hall and of the "spare chamber," or guest room, was patterned in soft brown which blended with the graining. The walls of Una's room were kalsomined in two shades of blue, separated by a narrow strip of black paper along which ran small gaily colored flowers. When Mrs. Hawthorne came to the problem of selecting fabrics for the new rooms, she showed skill in her choice of colors and materials. For the window seats in her little chapel she chose, in preference to chintz, a brocatelle with a claret ground and flower, which as she said, matched the carpet.

Details of the interior design, not usually found in this country, were the pointed arches over doors and windows in rooms which the Hawthornes added. Mr. Alcott, with his fondness for the Gothic, may have suggested the arches, or Mrs. Hawthorne may have seen similar ones abroad and adopted the idea for The Wayside. Marble mantels, popular at that time, were placed in two of the new rooms and in the library, which had formerly been part of the study. They were simple in

Mrs. Hawthorne's Parlor,
Hawthorne's Armchair at Left

line, Mrs. Hawthorne having carefully avoided the or-
nate design so often used in that period.

The process of completing and furnishing the additions was a lengthy one. Late in October Mr. Hawthorne told Mr. Longfellow at a meeting of the famous
Saturday Club, to which they both belonged, that he
was building a tower which he entered by a trap door
upon which he could place his chair when he wrote.
Even in December the lower rooms were not completed,
although Mr. Hawthorne mentioned in a letter that his
new study, which he later called his sky parlor, was
comfortable. The present steep stairway and sturdy door
with the pane of glass were undoubtedly added soon
after the lower rooms were finished, since Mr. Alcott
has mentioned that he never saw the trap door. A standing desk was later built at the suggestion of a relative
who thought that prolonged sitting was harmful to Mr.
Hawthorne's health. It has remained a characteristic
detail of the study although its owner did not use it to
any great extent, since he found that after giving it a
trial, he preferred to sit while he wrote.

As late as January, 1861, Mrs. Hawthorne wrote to
Mrs. James T. Fields of the slow progress in rebuilding:

> Ah me, we shall have order at some future day I
> dare to say. But now there is but one nook where we
> can take refuge from the Fury of Hubbab [*sic*]. This

nook is a wee Library, twelve by twelve! with book shelves on three sides, and on one side books upon them, while the other shelves open their mouths in vain for food. We thought we had more books, but we must now wait for slow accretions, as we have spent all we can on the house building. There will be one good feast soon perhaps for one openmouthed shelf—because Mr. Ticknor told Mr. Hawthorne he intended to send him a set of his Waverley Novels.

I am afraid we shall linger on in our finishings till spring—and I can do nothing pretty or nice till I can see clear spaces around me. Mr. Hawthorne enjoys his little library, but constantly laments its emptiness and proposes the funniest remedies—such as wooden rows, painted on the backs with immortal names—silk curtains carefully sheltering from dust *nothing at all!* all sorts of trash bound nicely with good titles. He is really getting demoralized you perceive, and begins to tolerate the idea of sham, he, the truest hater of sham I ever knew! But his desire for books is sapping his principles.

However, I will not talk nonsense any more. It is a darling little room and has the sun all day, and when the dining room is fit for Christians I hope you will come and spend a day at least. When we have a bedroom, I hope you will stay more than a day.

The prolonged rebuilding threatened to be a serious handicap to Mr. Hawthorne's work. The mounting costs were a cause of anxiety to him, the total expense proving to be approximately four times the original modest estimate. Another annoyance was the noise of the carpentry, naturally disturbing to one who, like Mr. Hawthorne, needed peace and quiet for his best efforts.

Always a steady worker, he chose the morning hours for his writing, and the afternoons for outdoor exercise. He preferred first to plan carefully what he later wrote, and was accustomed, as he meditated, to walk back and forth in the tower. The same thoughtful pacing was continued in the afternoon along his favorite hilltop path, which was bordered in spring by large light-blue violets, and from which he had an extensive view over his loved meadows. His daughter Rose has stated that he devoted himself constantly to writing, guarding his time, his temper, and his vitality, that he might give of his best.

The summer of 1860 was disturbed, not only by the noise and confusion of the carpentry, but by a return of illness to Una. At the time of her almost fatal attack in Rome, the Hawthornes had been warned that serious aftereffects might appear. In consequence, when she became ill, they were greatly alarmed until they found that she could be relieved by electrical treatments.

Mr. Hawthorne himself, while not visibly failing,

discovered that he did not have his old vigor. He, too, had been ill in Italy during the time that Una had wavered between life and death. Although he had apparently recovered, this illness and the subsequent worry about Una had combined to undermine his vitality. As he

Hawthorne's Seat on the Hilltop.   About 1880

himself remarked, his hair had become quite gray in Italy. After his return to The Wayside, his strength had for a time seemed to increase, but he never regained his original stamina.

One member of the family had not suffered from the years abroad. Julian, who had changed from a small boy of seven to an adolescent of fourteen, was a lively lad who required a good school. While the family was abroad, his father had grounded him well in Latin and Greek, with an unfailing patience and thoroughness; his mother and a governess had taught him history and literature; and in England he had been instructed in broadswords and other athletic skills. His father realized, nevertheless, that private lessons, however good the teacher might be, were by no means a substitute for the formal discipline of a well-organized academy. He, therefore, made arrangements for Julian to enter the excellent school which Mr. Sanborn had recently started for boys and girls.

Una, then sixteen, and Rose, who was eight, continued to receive their lessons at home, since their mother at that time preferred that they should not attend a co-educational school. Later Una had a tutor, Mr. George Bradford of Concord, the same teacher who in earlier years had given Anna Alcott a delightful introduction to the study of German.

The Hawthorne girls, although they did not attend

the school, went to the dances and other entertainments given by the pupils of the Sanborn school. A charming picture of life in Concord as it affected the Hawthorne young people is given by Una, then seventeen, in a letter to her aunt, Miss Elizabeth Palmer Peabody, dated June 5, 1861:

My dear Aunt Lizzie:

The books you sent have safely arrived, & Julian and I are delighted to see our dear old Arabian Nights again,—which, babyish as it may seem, we are going to read over again together whenever we have a chance.

I cannot think from whom you have heard of my playing, at any rate it was an entirely undeserved praise, because I do not play well, by which I understand the faultless execution of difficult & beautiful pieces. My acquirements merely consist in playing a few simple studies which can only give pleasure to my family, and at present I have not time to practise much, as I am studying with Mr. Bradford, who is an old friend of Papa's, and a very delightful teacher. I am reading Italian & Latin & studying arithmetic & Botany. I recite twice a week & enjoy it exceedingly. In the autumn I hope to join a drawing class composed of some of Mr. Sanborn's pupils, & then I shall be completely satisfied. Rose has

begun today to go to school, & is in the highest
spirits about it; so you see, all our educations are
being attended to at last. Rose goes to the East
Quarter Public School, where some of her friends
go, & it is kept by a very excellent lady to whom
Mamma feels quite happy to send her. Mr. Sanborn's school is farther off, & Mamma had several
reasons for not wanting her to go to that, besides.

Some of Mr. Sanborn's boys, Julian among the
rest, have been regularly drilling for the last few
weeks with a view to becoming soldiers, but the
other day [the] government sent for their guns which
it had provided them with, so they had to leave off,
but Julian says they think of going on without guns.
We were not at all sorry to have an end, as Julian
had to be called at five, go all the way down to the
armory which is more than a mile,—come back to
breakfast after the drill,—then return to school; &
as he comes back to dinner too it made him walk
about seven miles a day, which appeared to make
him too tired. It is rather to be regretted, on his
account especially, that we live so far from town.
I do not think Concord generally is a very healthy
place, but I think our house is in one of the best
situations, as it is high & sheltered & comparatively
dry, & is not so overshadowed by trees as the
Alcotts' & Emersons.' Neither has it any marshy

ground close to it, though there is a brook at the bottom of the opposite field. I am sure I ought to be well in it as it is my native air, and I am happy to say very well now, though I do not enjoy such an amount of exercise & occupation for its own sake as I should like to do. Our house is now entirely finished, & we are furnishing it at our leisure, & doing as much to our grounds and garden as Papa can afford, which is not a great deal. If we could keep a man all the time we could make a most lovely place of it.

Papa told me to say that as soon as our guest-chamber is prepared he depends upon your coming to pay us a good visit, and we want you to think about it and make up your mind, so as to be ready. Concord is a lovely place to visit, though it may not be so desirable to live in, & I think you would enjoy it very much. Do write & say you will come, before the weather gets very hot, because then there is not much enjoyment so far inland. But any time this month will be very pleasant.

Last Saturday we went to a pic-nic of Mr. Sanborn's scholars & their friends, & had a most charming time, rowing on Flint Pond, & walking about in the woods, & making flower wreaths. We drove there in carriages & waggons, & most of us drove back, but some had to walk because one of the horses broke down. I did not, however. I have a lesson to learn, dear Aunt Lizzie, so I must say goodbye, & hoping soon to hear from you a favorable reply to our invitation, I am

Your affectionate niece
Una Hawthorne

I wish I had some friend with whom I could read the Poets &c. because I find companionship & sympathy in such readings is very necessary to me, & I think I am old enough now to enjoy many of them very much. But as nobody seems at hand I suppose I must read by myself. I hoped you would like Mr. Motley's histories unqualifiedly. It seemed to me his style was not so picturesque as to take from the truth & exactness necessary to history, while its being so flowing & pleasant clothed the naked facts, as it were, & made them easier to remember, which is seldom the case in histories. But perhaps I am mistaken.

Both Mr. and Mrs. Hawthorne, constantly thoughtful for the welfare of their children, were determined that they should have full opportunity to join in the social life of the young people of the town. On one occasion, in creating a lovely gown decorated with sequins, which Una wore at a masquerade, Mrs. Hawthorne nearly exhausted herself by her long-continued sewing. Much to Julian's joy, his parents rented for him a costume in Boston, and he made a handsome appearance as the Earl of Leicester. At another time Una and Julian danced the old year out at a party in the Concord Town Hall.

Dances were also held at The Wayside. Mrs. Hawthorne in a letter to Mrs. James T. Fields, in June of 1862, delightfully described a party given for Una, at which forty guests were present. Although the rain had prevented Mrs. Fields and her husband from attending, fortunately it had not interfered with the "light, color, music and joy inside The Wayside."

> . . . I only wish you could have seen the groups of school girls—so pretty as they all were with rosy cheeks and laughing eyes & lovely rich braided hair and bouquets of brilliant flowers in their hands and boddices [*sic*]. We took every rag of furniture out of the dining room and Julian's room on each side the chapel, and the library (except chairs and one table) so that there might be room for five sets of dancers. We received in the drawing room, where there was to be no dancing. The whole house on the lower piano was dressed with Roses the rarest roses from Mrs. Emerson's choice bushes—and from Mr. Bull's immense variety of the finest specimens.

Mrs. Hawthorne added that her husband came down

from "his high estate in the Tower, and looked, in the gay throng, like a grand Olympian, descended to a 'Paradise of Children' in a golden age." She continued:

> . . . Many of them had never seen him, and were glad enough, and greatly surprised—and at the end, they tried to get up courage to go and bid him good night. My niece told me that she heard one young lady say "Oh how I want to shake hands with Mr. Hawthorne but I am afraid" Judge Hoar's son said "Oh don't be afraid—I am going to. It is proper and he is not a bear. He will not bite." So Sam Hoar came in and did his duty, and then a piquant, vivid looking girl followed, and several took courage as well—and they all got hospitable smiles, and seemed hugely pleased.

In addition to these more formal affairs, there were skating and other neighborhood good times for the young people. Mrs. Hawthorne herself kept up her friendship with the Concord ladies, who often walked down to see her on her official day at home, Wednesday. The Alcotts and the Hawthornes went to each other's houses, sometimes for tea, sometimes to play whist, act in charades, or write impromptu verse. Although Mr. Hawthorne was not apt to enter into these festivities, yet, as we have seen, he would upon occasion join the young people. As an example of his ability to write impromptu verse, we have the well-known lines about Alcott, the vegetarian, at "Apple Slump," Louisa's nickname for Orchard House.

> *There dwelt a Sage at Apple-Slump,*
> *Whose dinner never made him plump;*
> *Give him carrots, potatoes, squash, parsnips, and peas,*
> *And some boiled macaroni, without any cheese,*
> *And a plate of raw apples to hold on his knees,*
> *And a glass of sweet cider, to wash down all these,—*
> *And he'd prate of the Spirit as long as you'd please,—*
> *This airy Sage of Apple-Slump!* [5]

One form of entertainment into which the family entered with special pleasure was listening to Mr. Hawthorne read aloud. In the little library they sat around the center table, Mrs. Hawthorne at one end with a basket of sewing before her. Mr. Hawthorne, settled in his comfortable chair, usually held the book in his left hand, his fingers over the top of the page to keep the volume open. As he read, a slight forward motion of his head gave emphasis to the words. Julian has written that the motion of his father's head was not disturbing to the listeners, but rather made clear the "constant living *rapport* between him and the author." Further describing the scene, Julian wrote, "All the characters

---

[5] Julian Hawthorne, *Nathaniel Hawthorne and His Wife* (1885), II, 322.

seemed to live and move visibly before us," adding with reference to his father, "The expression of his face changed, as he read, in harmony with the speech or the passage."[6]

The young people would postpone any other form of entertainment in order to hear their father read aloud from the Waverley novels. These books had been favorites of Mr. Hawthorne in his boyhood, and when abroad he had taken special pleasure in visiting Sir Walter Scott's home, Abbotsford. Perhaps for that reason he was particularly pleased when Ticknor and Fields dedicated to him their Household Edition of Lockhart's *Life of Sir Walter Scott*. In a letter to Mr. Hawthorne, February 25, 1861, Mr. Fields wrote that he had decided upon the dedication after reading aloud "Artist of the Beautiful," from *Mosses from an Old Manse*. The happy relations between these two men, the publisher and the author, is evidenced in Mr. Hawthorne's reply:

> I am exceedingly gratified by the dedication. I do not deserve so high an honor; but if you think me worthy, it is enough to make the compliment in the highest degree acceptable, no matter who may dispute my title to it. I care more for your good opinion than for that of a host of critics, and have an excellent reason for so doing; inasmuch as my

[6] *Ibid*, II, 9.

literary success, whatever it has been or may be, is the result of my connection with you. Somehow or other you smote the rock of public sympathy on my behalf, and a stream gushed forth in sufficient quantity to quench my thirst though not to drown me. I think no author can ever have had publisher that he valued so much as I do mine.[7]

Shortly before the publication of the biography, the Waverley novels had been issued in the Household Edition. A set had been bound especially for Mrs. Hawthorne, whose delight in the beautiful books was mentioned by her husband in a letter to Mr. Ticknor. Mr. Hawthorne added, "and I myself took very great pleasure in arranging them on the shelf."[8] He used this set of the Waverley novels when he read aloud to his attentive family, grouped around the center table in the cozy little library.

Life in The Wayside could not maintain itself always at this lighthearted level. The Civil War began and, at about the same time, Mr. Hawthorne showed definite signs of ill health. As early as May, 1861, he was obliged to cancel an engagement with Mr. Lowell because of illness. Realizing the physical and mental benefit which he gained from a change of scene, espe-

---

[7] James T. Fields, *Yesterdays with Authors* (1872), p. 102.
[8] Caroline Ticknor, *Hawthorne and His Publisher* (1913), p. 256.

cially to the seashore, he made a number of trips, one at least with Una and several with Julian, who was becoming each year more companionable. Although Mr. Hawthorne enjoyed such trips with his son, he was never long happy away from his wife and two daughters, Una, or "Onion" as he affectionately called her, and Rose, or "Bab," who was ten years old when he wrote to her the following letter:

Pride's Crossing,
West Beach,
Beverley Farms,
August 5th, 1861

Dear Bab

This Monday morning is a little cooler than any morning for a week past; and I am truly thankful, for it seems to me as if I never knew what hot weather is, until this experience. I feel as if I had been (to borrow Una's expression about the Concord soldiers) "through Purgatory, *at least*." The sea itself seemed to reflect heat, as though it were made of hot molten metal. I am afraid you have all suffered very much, and that I shall find you reduced to a crisp on my return.

Owing to this hot weather, we have taken no long walks, but merely a stroll to the beach, in the morning and evening; and the rest of the time, we betake ourselves to the shadiest part of the woods, and gather such berries as are within our reach. There are much finer huckleberries than on our hill, besides blackberries, and high bush blueberries, which are very good—only not worth the trouble of picking in such awful weather.

Tell Mamma that I see no newspapers, and do not know, at this moment, whether the Rebels have taken Washington, or what other misfortune may have happened. Almost every hour, however, I hear the noise of drums, over the water, from Marblehead or Salem, and very often the thunder of cannon, which sometimes continues for an hour together; so that I begin to think the war has overspread the whole country except just this little precinct in the neighborhood of West Beach. On the whole, I enjoy this respite from the daily repetition and contradiction of telegraphs about skirmishes, victories, and defeats, and could almost be content to remain in the same ignorance till the war is over. . . .

Julian and I are both very well; and he does not seem to have suffered so much from the heat as I have. I have great trouble to keep his appetite within due bounds, and to rescue Mrs. Pierce's pies and tarts from his insatiable maw; but he is a very good boy, and quite amiable when sufficiently fed. . . .

Dear Bab, I am very homesick, and have come to

the conclusion that when a person has a comfortable home of his own, and a a [*sic*] good little Bab of his own, and a good great Onion, and a best mamma, he had better stay with them than roam abroad. Thank Heaven, we shall return on Saturday.

Your affectionate Father.

A journey which gave him special pleasure was one in 1862 taken in company with Mr. Ticknor. From New York Mr. Hawthorne wrote happily of going with his friend to the Century Club where he met various artists and literary people. While in Washington he visited his trusted college friend, Horatio Bridge, then paymaster general in charge of a naval bureau. Mr. Hawthorne's stay in Washington was a great success. Shortly after visiting Manassas and Fortress Munroe, he wrote to his wife, "I have now seen almost everything of interest in and about Washington, and begin to long for home. It has done me a great deal of good, this constant activity of mind and body, but being perfectly well, I no longer need it as a medicine." In the midst of excursions to places made important by the war, Mr. Hawthorne took time to write a long letter to Julian giving all the details which he knew would entertain a boy of sixteen. His keen and affectionate understanding of his son can be seen in every line of the letter.

When Mr. Hawthorne returned to The Wayside, he wrote of his experiences in the thoughtful article, "Chiefly about War Matters," which appeared in the *Atlantic Monthly* for July, 1862. The horrors of the Civil War, although they did not directly touch Mr. Hawthorne's family, were never far from his consciousness. They crept even into some stanzas which he and Una once improvised together, each composing, as Julian explained later, two lines of a verse.

> *Oh snow that comes*
> *When violets ought to bloom!*
> *Oh thunderous drums*
> *That lead man to the tomb!*

> *Oh doleful robin*
> *On from warmer climes!*
> *Oh wretched bobbin!*
> *Suiting alone my rhymes!*

> *Oh heat that vainly strives*
> *To dry up mud!*
> *Oh myriad of young & happy lives,*
> *Untimely quenched by rebel hands in blood*

> *So must the virtuous look*
> *To higher spheres!*
> *Although the little brook*
> *Be swelled with tears!*

Although Mr. Hawthorne wrote steadily in his tower during these years, *Our Old Home* was the only work he published. It was a series of articles on his experiences in England, printed first in the *Atlantic*, but not put into book form until 1863. As each article appeared, his good friend, Mr. James T. Fields, the junior partner of the publishing firm, who was also editor of the *Atlantic*, would jubilantly report the acclaim with which it was received by Mr. Longfellow, Mr. Lowell, or Dr. Holmes. Later when the time arrived to decide upon the dedication of the book, Mr. Hawthorne wrote to Mr. Fields that he wished to acknowledge the great kindness which Mr. Francis Bennoch had shown him in England, but that he was indebted to Franklin Pierce for his appointment to the consulship at Liverpool and therefore ought to take this opportunity to honor him. When the news reached his friends that he considered dedicating his new book to the former President, whose prewar policies regarding the slavery question had met with bitter opposition in the North, a storm of protest arose. Mr. Hawthorne was told that his reputation would suffer and, what is difficult for an author to face, that his book would have no market. Mr. Fields, usually so receptive to any suggestion made by Mr. Hawthorne, wrote on July 15, 1863, that in the opinion of book sellers the dedication would ruin the sale of the book. One dealer had refused to order even a single copy, although his customers were admirers of Mr. Hawthorne's books.

Mr. Hawthorne took time to consider the matter fully, but his final decision was a victory for his loyalty to Franklin Pierce. At the top of the manuscript of his dedicatory letter are the words, written in large letters, "To a Friend." As he wrote in the letter, Franklin Pierce had been his friend for many years and still was his friend; to him, therefore, as a personal friend he dedicated the book. Nor was his loyalty misplaced. Mr. Pierce was always tender and devoted even to the last day of Mr. Hawthorne's life. As for the dire prophecies, they did not materialize. The book sold well, although a few persons, among them Mr. Emerson, cut the dedication from their copies. On the whole Mr. Hawthorne's friends admired his courage and they forgave what they felt was the perversity of his choice.

Another book written during these years, but not published until later, was *Septimius Felton*. It was based upon a legend, told to Hawthorne by Thoreau, that a former owner of the house had believed his spirit would never die. In a note for the story Hawthorne wrote:

Begin with a reference to a certain room in my house, which I hint to be haunted; or to be remarkable and interesting to us for certain occult reasons. —Leave the matter thus, for the present, and diverge to a description of the hill and ground generally, the distant village, where the clock is heard to strike. . . .

He added that he would mention Mr. Alcott and Mr. Bull with his grapes and would refer to the battle cry and the soldiers on the hill.

> Then come to the annals of the house, and introduce Thoreau's legend of the man who would not die. Make the impression about the room, or chamber, more striking and begin to connect this legend with the particular locality of the house. . . .

He later identified the room as the east bedroom, the one near whose chimney is the hiding place already mentioned.

During these years Mr. Hawthorne visited his friends in Boston from time to time. He would often drop in at the office of his publishers in their shop, the Old Corner Bookstore. There he might chat with Mr. Fields in his little curtained corner where a group of authors were apt to congregate. More often he would ensconce himself in a favorite armchair in a secluded corner of Mr. Ticknor's counting room, which was elevated a few steps above the level of the store. Thus all that happened in the store was open to his keen observation, yet he could retire into quiet meditation when he wished to do so.

Although he avoided formal entertainments, he occasionally attended some of the Saturday Club meetings, those delightful two o'clock dinners held the last Saturday of each month in the upper front room of the Parker House. Oftentimes the members would sit at table for four hours, enjoying the witty and learned conversation of such men as Holmes, Agassiz, Whittier, Longfellow, and Emerson. Hawthorne usually played the role of listener, but his occasional trenchant remarks, as at official dinners in London, often clarified a long discussion. By the time these meetings had ended, the last train to Concord had departed, although a later one ran as far as Waltham, halfway to the destination of Mr. Hawthorne and Mr. Emerson. The difficulty was solved by the third member, Judge Ebenezer Rockwood Hoar, father of the Sam Hoar who had braved Mr. Hawthorne at Una's dancing party. Judge Hoar arranged that his own man, driving the carryall and the big black horse, should meet them at the Waltham station. Thus these three men, so interesting to each other, had an opportunity for a quiet chat while they jogged along the cool country road after the heavy dinner and long conversation. Perhaps Judge Hoar and Mr. Hawthorne might seldom have met otherwise, so chary was Mr. Hawthorne of interruptions to his writing.

A fund of common sense, great kindliness, and almost hidden humor, at once subtle and homely, won for Mr. Hawthorne regard and deep affection. Several charming letters passed between him and James Russell Lowell concerning visits to Elmwood, or to The Wayside. Mr. Lowell ended an especially delightful letter, May 24, 1863, with these words:

> Now will you write and say when you are to be expected? I assure you I have looked forward to your coming as one of my chiefest spring pleasures, ranking it with the advent of the birds.

With Mr. Lowell, Mr. Hawthorne found a quiet, but real companionship. When Mr. Lowell gave his publishers a list of friends to whom copies of the new book, *Conversations on Some of the Old Poets,* should be sent, he wrote opposite Hawthorne's name, "with author's love." Lowell was the friend who, in 1860, had written the humorous note introducing young William Dean Howells, who in *Literary Friends and Acquaintance* has given us a charming description of his visit to The Wayside and Mr. Hawthorne's understanding kindness to the shy young man.

There were other friends who came to The Wayside, and with whom Mr. Hawthorne could quietly discuss matters of mutual interest. Mr. Franklin Pierce and Mr. and Mrs. James T. Fields were always eagerly awaited. Mr. Hawthorne wrote several times to his old friend, Mr. Horatio Bridge, asking him and his wife to stop en route to their summer home in northern New England. Others have described Mr. Hawthorne's cordiality and companionship during their visits at The Wayside: Mr. Edward Dicey of England, Miss Rebecca Harding of Virginia, and, a favorite in the Hawthorne family, Miss Mary A. Dodge, better known to us under her pen name, "Gail Hamilton." To entertain such visitors the Hawthornes sometimes invited Mr. Emerson and Mr. Alcott to a midday dinner. Rambles through the woods and over the hills to the Old Manse or to Walden Pond, in the opposite direction, also provided diversion.

Hawthorne's Desk, Bookcase, and Chair
in Mrs. Hawthorne's Little "Chapel"

More intimate neighborhood friendliness was not forgotten, especially by Mrs. Hawthorne. She had by nature a simple kindliness which took account of her neighbors' welfare and preoccupations, whether those neighbors were Mr. and Mrs. Robert Browning in Italy, or Mr. and Mrs. Alcott at Orchard House. With the Alcotts her relations had always been friendly from the early days before her marriage when for a short time she had joined her sister, Elizabeth Palmer Peabody, as a teacher in Mr. Alcott's school in Boston. Such had been the affection between the Alcotts and Miss Elizabeth Peabody that they had named their third daughter for her. This friendliness between the families was renewed in Concord. Soon after the return of the Hawthornes Mr. Alcott described in his diary an evening spent at The Wayside, when Mr. Hawthorne showed "numerous sterreopic [*sic*] views of England, Rome, Paris & Florence, and H. tells me of the Club meeting yesterday at the Parker House, Emerson, Agassiz, Holmes &c." Homemade gifts, as well as visits, were exchanged between the two houses. Apples and cider were presents from Mr. Alcott, his wife often sending some of her beer made from spruce sprigs, hops, and a little molasses. Mr. Alcott recorded in his diary, January 1, 1861, "The Hawthornes send us a bread-dish of carved wood ornamented with wheat-ears, and very pretty." Two years later he wrote to Mrs. Hawthorne as follows:

Dear Mrs. Hawthorne

Thanks for the restored Shade. It is as beautiful as it will be useful. Certainly nothing could be more scholarly. I shall set it in the centre of my study table, and associate the Givers with the Arts and Graces whose radiance they have contrived to mellow for my pleasure.

When next in the city, I will see if I can find a picture worthy of the acceptance of Rose and Mr. Hawthorne.

Truly yours
A. Bronson Alcott

Friday Morning
  April 10 1863

The first Christmas after the Hawthornes' return, Louisa made a holly wreath for the new tower study. On the occasion of her thirtieth birthday on November 29, 1862 she received presents from The Wayside and acknowledged them in a delightful poem, entitled "The Hawthorne Tree," in which she recounted her pleasure in the remembrances. Shortly afterward when she was summoned to serve as a nurse in the army hospital in Georgetown, she was assisted in her hurried preparations by Mrs. Hawthorne, who marked her clothing and offered to do anything else which might be of help. During the anxious weeks which followed her departure,

Mrs. Hawthorne kept the little family in the Orchard House in mind, on one occasion during the holiday season asking them to tea. In a letter to Mrs. James T. Fields, Mrs. Hawthorne herself has described the little party and the arrival home of Una who had been on a visit.

It was very pleasant to have a Christmas tree to greet Una upon her return to us. Her own happy face, as she burst in upon us was the best of it. We had Mr. and Mrs. Alcott and their daughter Abby to tea, and our little party just filled the chapel. On the tip of the tree was a little angel holding in one hand a golden shining world, and in the other a scroll upon which was written, "Peace on Earth, Good Will to Men." Round the trunk wound a serpent, and upon all the branches hung and glittered the goods and toys of life. There was nothing costly, but it was quite pretty with a little contrivance and more painstaking.

Very soon Louisa was taken desperately ill and was brought back to the Orchard House. During the days when the question as to whether or not she would live was a grave one, all of the Alcotts' friends rallied to their aid. Mrs. Hawthorne insisted, among other things, that Abba should have her meals at The Wayside so that she might be for at least part of each day in cheerful surroundings.

Mrs. Hawthorne's genuine interest in Louisa is perhaps shown most clearly in connection with a poem of Louisa's, written after the death of Henry Thoreau. The verses had come to Louisa one midnight in the hospital at Georgetown, while she was sitting by the bedside of a dying lad. After her return to Concord, she read the poem to her father, as he has mentioned in his diary. He, in turn, read it to Mr. and Mrs. Hawthorne. They, much impressed, spoke of it to Mr. Fields. Later, after securing it from Louisa, Mrs. Hawthorne made a copy and sent it to Mrs. Fields, an act of friendly appreciation which gave to *Atlantic* readers the tender poem, "Flutes."

Of all Mrs. Hawthorne's friends the one with whom she was most intimate was Mrs. Fields. It is indeed from her letters to this wise and generous friend that I have gained much of my information in regard to the daily interests and activities of the family. Mrs. Hawthorne felt that she could speak freely about whatever was uppermost at the moment: her own theories on life, especially her religious beliefs, the details of dresses she was making for Rose, her fear that Julian was not sufficiently practical to succeed in a practical world, her devoted care of a young girl who had lost her sister under tragic circumstances, the fair that was going to be held in Concord to raise money for Negro orphan children. In regard to the last subject, Mrs. Hawthorne remarked that for five weeks the fair had taken all her spare time and that of the three young people. She explained that Rose, in preparation for it, was to "make a book of the Life of Penelope from Flaxman—and I am to illuminate the cover for her." Both girls painted vases, paper knives, and baskets. Julian made an illumination on vellum of two verses of Tennyson's "Ring out, wild bells," decorating it with his own designs. Mrs. Hawthorne herself made "a book of the old Rhyme of Gaffer Grey—putting the text into German letters, and illustrating it in outline from the old prints as well as from my own notions." Altogether, their efforts produced one hundred dollars for the fair.

Often Mrs. Hawthorne visited at the home of Mrs. Fields on Charles Street in Boston, and then she revelled in the long talks with her understanding and charming friend. The Hawthorne children, too, were at the Fields so often that their house became almost a second home to them. Once Julian arrived at The Wayside, clad in a fine new raincoat provided by Mr. Fields, who had refused to let him return unprotected in the face of a bad storm. Both Mr. and Mrs. Fields were ever generous and thoughtful, sending frequent gifts to The Wayside. In this and in many other ways they fully deserved the names of "Heartsease" and "Mrs. Meadows," which Mrs. Hawthorne and the children affectionately gave them.

At their house Mr. Hawthorne could rest as in no other place away from his own home. Mrs. Fields's sympathetic and happy spirit put the shy man at ease. Her husband was an intimate friend, to whom Mr. Hawthorne turned for complete understanding, whether on a literary topic or a problem of the universe. His regret was deep when, at the beginning of 1864, his failing health forced him to refuse invitations even to so sheltering a home.

Gradual loss of strength seriously affected Mr. Hawthorne's writing. During the last few years of his life he spent especially long hours in his study, writing and rewriting, almost as if he realized that his productive days were numbered and wished to accomplish all that his waning strength allowed. Satisfied only with his best, he did not publish *Septimius Felton,* although he had laboriously completed two versions, the cramped handwriting of which shows the physical effort he had made. In the latter part of 1863 he was at work on *The Dolliver Romance,* which was to be published as a serial in the *Atlantic Monthly.* Contrary to his usual custom, he allowed an announcement to be made before the book was completed. In the first months of 1864, when it became evident that he must delay further chapters, and therefore the publication of the serial, he wrote to Mr. Fields suggesting various whimsical excuses which might be offered to the *Atlantic* readers. These whimsical excuses, with many other letters of Mr. Hawthorne, have been given to us by Mr. Fields in his delightful biographical sketch of Mr. Hawthorne in *Yesterdays with Authors.*

In the early months of 1864 Mr. Hawthorne's health rapidly became worse. Mrs. Hawthorne, alarmed at the seriousness of his condition, urged that he have medical care; but he was averse to consulting a physician. Since earlier trips either to the seashore or to cities had seemed to revive him, it was arranged late in March, 1864, that he should travel under the care of Mr. Ticknor to New York and possibly farther south. Bonds of friendship between the two men were so close that Mr. Ticknor was ready to undertake the journey in spite of the cold from which he was suffering. The tragic sequel is well known. Mr. Ticknor, to protect Mr. Hawthorne on a chilly and unexpectedly long drive, gave his overcoat to the invalid. The result was the intensification of Mr. Ticknor's cold and his sudden death in Philadelphia. For Mr. Hawthorne the shock was intense. His wife wrote to Mrs. Fields a few days after his return:

> He came back unlooked-for that day . . . as soon as I saw his face I was frightened out of all knowledge of myself—so haggard, so white, so deeply scored with pain and fatigue was the face—so much more ill he looked than I ever saw him before. He had walked from the station because he saw no carriage there, and his brow was streaming with a perfect rain —so great had been the effort to walk so far.[9]

---

[9] Quoted from the MS. Reprinted also in Fields, *op. cit.*, pp. 118–119.

Mrs. Hawthorne nursed him as best she could, but realized that something further must be done for him. Since he now had a horror of trains and cities, Mr. Pierce offered to take him on a slow driving trip through New Hampshire and possibly into Maine, stopping at whatever places pleased them. Preparations were made, and Mr. Hawthorne went to Boston, accompanied by his wife, who wrote that he was not well enough to be left by himself, but that she trusted Mr. Pierce's skilled and affectionate care. The travelers commenced their leisurely trip, and, by easy stages, reached Plymouth, on May 18. That was the last stop. In the early hours of the following morning Mr. Hawthorne peacefully passed from sleep into death.

The news was brought to The Wayside by Mr. Emerson. Mr. Fields immediately came to see Mrs. Hawthorne and later made the arrangements for the funeral, which was held in the Unitarian Church in Concord. Spring flowers were everywhere, but close beside Mr. Hawthorne were his favorite lilies of the valley. On the casket was placed the unfinished chapter of *The Dolliver Romance,* upon which he had done his last work. In *Yesterdays with Authors* Mr. Fields has written:

On the 24th of May we carried Hawthorne through the blossoming orchards of Concord, and laid him down under a group of pines, on a hillside, overlooking historic fields. All the way from the village church to the grave the birds kept up a perpetual melody. The sun shone brightly, and the air was sweet and pleasant, as if death had never entered the world. Longfellow and Emerson, Channing and Hoar, Agassiz and Lowell, Greene and Whipple, Alcott and Clarke, Holmes and Hillard, and other friends whom he loved, walked slowly by his side that beautiful spring morning. The companion of his youth and his manhood, for whom he would willingly, at any time, have given up his life, Franklin Pierce, was there among the rest and scattered flowers into the grave.[10]

The beauty and peace of that spring day are in the lines by Mr. Longfellow beginning:

> *How beautiful it was, that one bright day*
> *In the long week of rain!*
> *Though all its splendor could not chase away*
> *The omnipresent pain.*
>
> *The lovely town was white with apple-blooms,*
> *And the great elms o'erhead*
> *Dark shadows wove on their aerial looms,*
> *Shot through with golden thread.*[11]

---

[10] *Ibid.*, p. 124.
[11] "Hawthorne," May 23, 1864.

After Mr. Hawthorne's death the house seemed empty, shorn of his smile and of his guiding spirit. Mrs. Hawthorne in a letter to Mr. Longfellow thanking him for his tender poem about the funeral wrote:

> I cannot suppose that you would wish, now that All is gone, to come to this house, no longer a palace since the king has left it. But if you are ever in Concord, and would not feel too much saddened to enter these deserted halls, I should most gladly welcome you as one of his chief friends, tenderly valued. His visits to you in Cambridge used to be a great enjoyment to him. He always spoke of them as peculiarly agreeable.[12]

Mrs. Hawthorne's acceptance of her tragic loss, however, showed fine courage. On the day the news arrived, Una wrote to Mrs. Fields:

> Mr. Fields will tell you about Mamma. Nothing could be imagined more angelically lovely. It is a triumph of the most vivid faith I ever saw.

Mrs. Hawthorne's belief in the goodness of God and in eternal life was unfaltering. She did not rail against her loss; she thanked God for the wonderful gift of her husband's perfect love; she was comforted by the thought that her weary beloved had been given rest and peace;

---

[12] *Life of Henry Wadsworth Longfellow*, edited by Samuel Longfellow (1886), II, 471.

she was sustained by her belief that the short time on earth remaining to her was to be followed by eternal life and reunion with her husband. Even on earth she felt his spiritual presence, and wrote, "I am so near the ascended one, that I shall not fail to know his counsel."

Mrs. Hawthorne did not allow herself to become self-absorbed. She maintained her balance, and in the midst of her own grief often expressed both by word and deed keen sympathy for others in sorrow: for cousins whose eldest child had died, and for Mrs. Fields whose brother had been reported "missing" in the war. Her chief concern, however, was for her children and for her husband's remaining manuscripts. She wrote:

> I have as much as I can do now to keep quiet and preserve a mood of cheer for the children. I could not separate myself from them to do anything. My duty is to them and for them I live.

For their sakes she took up the difficult problem of finances, which always perplexed her. She strove to conform to the requirements which were necessarily imposed upon her by the executor of her husband's will, his good friend, the lawyer, George S. Hillard. Mr. Hawthorne's estate was valued at over twenty-six thousand dollars, in addition to his house and land, but cash was needed for inheritance taxes and for current living expenses. There were many manuscripts, some of which might be suitable for early publication. Here was a task which appealed to Mrs. Hawthorne, and for which she was well fitted.

The manuscript material needed careful reading and much of it required copying. Some was on loose sheets, and all was written in so minute a hand that it was difficult to decipher. Mrs. Hawthorne at once started to transcribe what she found, sending to Mr. Fields the parts which she thought might be interesting to readers of the *Atlantic Monthly.* It was a labor of love, albeit an exacting one, but she found comfort in the close association with her husband's handwriting. Many, however, are her letters to Mr. Fields in which she expressed her fear that something would be published which, unaccompanied by adequate explanation, might harm her husband's reputation.

Mr. Hawthorne had personally been known to comparatively few persons, and naturally there arose among his readers a desire to learn more about him. It was at first proposed that Mrs. Hawthorne write a biography. Such intrusion into the citadel of Mr. Hawthorne's inner life was abhorrent to her. She wrote:

> Details are not for him. The effect of his character, though so hidden from actual sight—will be felt as long as his books last. It was the only way he chose to present himself to the world.

She had already decided: "I can neither write a book, nor

could I, if able, so entirely act in opposition to my husband's express wish and opinion as to do so."

Although the proposal for the biography was dropped,
there arose the question of Mr. Hawthorne's notebooks,
which he had kept for his own use and pleasure. It was
finally decided that they should be given to the public,
first in the *Atlantic Monthly*, and then in book form. Mrs.
Hawthorne was glad that they were to be published
under the supervision of Mr. Fields; her trust in his
judgment and loyalty was profound. She wrote to him:

> I thank Heaven and have for years thanked Heaven
> for allotting to my husband such friends for pub-
> lishers, as you and Mr. Ticknor have been. The
> repose, the confidence, the satisfaction and admira-
> tion he has always felt in regard to your care of him
> and his interests have helped to illumine his life. . . .
> Together we have so often rejoiced over you, and
> congratulated ourselves at the kind Providence that
> led him to you.

Nevertheless, Mrs. Hawthorne felt keenly her own
responsibility towards the manuscripts which her husband
had not prepared for publication. In her anxiety to protect his memory, she occasionally changed certain words
and phrases which she thought might give a wrong impression of his delicacy of thought, or which she considered broke some rule of rhetoric. The actual labor of

copying the American notebooks was long and arduous, and many times her eyes failed her when she pored for hours over the fine cramped handwriting. Yet with all her toil and sense of responsibility, she felt that thereby she came closer to him. In her letters to Mrs. Fields she mentions this feeling of companionship.

The children, too, missed the bright presence of their father; their feeling of loss is best expressed in Rose's book, *Memories of Hawthorne,* "We have missed him in the sunshine, in the storm, in the twilight, ever since." In order to come as close to him as they could, they decided to read his books again. Mrs. Hawthorne wrote:

> We began last evening at "the Grey Champion" and the children are going to read me aloud all the works from first to last in the evenings. Will not this be a fair monument to his beloved memory—fairer than St. Paul's to Christopher Wren?

It must have been a charming family group, the handsome boy just coming into manhood, the two beautiful daughters with the gorgeous red-gold hair, and the grey-haired woman who had been a real helpmate to her husband.

A delightful description of the family about this time has been given by Col. Thomas Wentworth Higginson, who visited The Wayside in 1867. Una opened the door. Her face and eyes were what he had anticipated, but her figure and port surprised him by their nobility. He wrote, "Her magnificent hair blazed and glittered upon me...most unexpectedly."[13] Rose, whose exquisite complexion was framed by hair as golden red as Una's, sang "dreamy and thoughtful songs" for them in the evening, and later pale-faced Mrs. Hawthorne sat on a low chair and talked to him of her husband.

After their father's death, the young people seemed suddenly to grow up. Una was a young lady, and undertook to help the family finances by teaching gymnastics. Rose, whose thirteenth birthday came at the time of her father's death, was, for a year or so, a student at a nearby boarding school in Lexington. Julian was attending Harvard College, walking the fifteen miles from Cambridge, now and again, to spend a week end with his family. On one such occasion, when he was returning from a sailing expedition, he arrived home about midnight, famished, and therefore dismayed to discover that the house was dark and empty. He obtained entrance, however, by climbing a waterspout to an upper window. In the kitchen all of the food had been put away. He wondered how he could exist until morning, knowing well that, even if he walked the mile to the village, all stores would be shut at that time of night. Then he remembered that sometimes pies were placed in the little closet under the

---

[13] *Letters and Journals of Thomas Wentworth Higginson*, edited by Mary Thacher Higginson (Houghton Mifflin Company, 1921), p. 238.

stairs. More than sixty years afterwards, when he told me the story, a beaming smile encircled his face as he said, "And there were *fourteen* pies!"

Various difficulties, illness, and other disappointments beset the Hawthornes. It was finally decided in 1868 that they should again go abroad, this time to Germany so that Julian might complete his engineering education. Since their return was uncertain, The Wayside was offered for sale. Mrs. Hawthorne did not again return to the United States; and Una made only one short visit. They both died in England, Mrs. Hawthorne in 1871 and Una in 1877, and are buried at Kensal Green.

In 1870 the house with about nineteen acres of land was purchased by Abba Gray, wife of George Gray of Concord, and was the home of their family for two years. In 1872, when they moved to a new house which they had built across the road from the old barn, they retained the land on the south side of the highway. Before they left The Wayside, their son, Arthur, decorated the ceiling of the tower in memory of Mr. Hawthorne. The frescoes which he painted on the ceiling are still to be seen there.

The next owner, Miss Mary Pratt, brought to the old house her boarding school for girls, which she named "The Wayside Family School." It was small and home-like, maintaining happy relations with Concord residents.

A few of the girls of the town, and at least three boys, attended as day scholars. Two of the boys were sons of Anna Alcott, *Little Women's* Meg, who in 1860 had become Mrs. John Pratt. Concord provided at least one of the teachers, Mrs. Ripley Bartlett, who has told me that the two lower rooms were used as class or study rooms, and that she herself taught in the little room with the bay window, the one which Mrs. Hawthorne had earlier called her chapel. The tower was a bedroom for three of the girls.

The school's connection with Concord was not limited to the instruction of some of its young people; the townspeople were invited to several fetes, for one of which, held June 18, 1874, William Ellery Channing wrote a poem, entitled "Happy School Days." For the occasion Chinese lanterns illuminated the larch path, hillside, and the lawn, where the prizes and diplomas were presented, and where later the young people danced. Mr. Alcott, who lived next door in Orchard House, wrote in his diary, describing the event:

> It is a picturesque spectacle, the shrubbery glimmering from the boughs contrasting with the white dresses of the young ladies, and illuminating the faces of the gay company. Hawthorne simply must have ventured to bestow a shy glance upon the scene from his haunts, or delegated his ghost, if too coy himself.

Both upon that occasion and at the last commencement in 1879, Mr. Alcott presented the diplomas and congratulated the girls upon their good fortune in having studied in Mr. Hawthorne's old home.

Even before the close of the last school year, The Wayside had returned to the possession of a Hawthorne. It had been purchased by George Parsons Lathrop, who had married Rose Hawthorne. To it they brought their little son, Francis Hawthorne Lathrop, then two years old. Perhaps his mother recalled that she had been the same age when she left The Wayside on her first trip abroad, twenty-six years earlier. Francis was a healthy,

The Wayside from the West. About 1885

happy child, full of spirit. He loved to have his father swing him into the air. "Put me way up—way up in the blue sky," he would beg. After the little boy's sudden death from diphtheria, February 6, 1881, Mr. Lathrop wrote the poem.

THE CHILD'S WISH GRANTED

Do.you remember, my sweet absent son,
How in the soft June days forever done
You loved the heavens so warm and clear and high;
And when I lifted you, soft came your cry—
"Put me 'way up—'way 'way up in blue sky."

I laughed and said I could not—put you down,
Your grey eyes wonderfilled beneath that crown
Of bright hair gladdening me as you raced by.
Another Father now, more strong than I,
Has borne you voiceless to your dear blue sky.[14]

At the time of little Francis's death, the Lathrops were spending the winter in Boston, where Mr. Lathrop had been giving a course of lectures entitled, "Symbolism of Color in Nature, Art, Literature and Life." Saddened by their loss, the Lathrops could not bear to live again at The Wayside.

The house was not long to remain vacant, for it was

---

[14] George Parsons Lathrop, *Dreams and Days* (Charles Scribner's Sons, 1892), p. 131.

needed the next winter by the family of Julian Hawthorne, Mrs. Lathrop's brother. He was remaining in
Europe for a few months, but his wife with their six
children returned to this country and lived in The Wayside for the winter of 1881-1882. Again Hawthorne
children ran through the halls and along the terraces.
One of these children was Miss Hildegarde Hawthorne,
now well known to young people through her biogra-
phies of her grandfather and some of his friends. She has
told me of happy memories when, as a little girl, she
and her brother Jack coasted down the path by the terraces or played about the brook, where their father had
had such fun with his turtles when he was a boy.

The Lothrops and the
Five Little Peppers

Underwood & Underwood

MRS. DANIEL LOTHROP [*as a young woman*]

MRS. DANIEL LOTHROP

DANIEL LOTHROP

arly in the spring of 1883 the Lathrops decided to sell The Wayside and advertised it in a Boston newspaper. The happy chance by which my father, Daniel Lothrop, noticed the advertisement and immediately secured an option on the property has already been described. It was fitting that this house of rich literary associations should now become the home of another author and her husband, a publisher. It was particularly fitting that two lovers of children, Mr. Alcott and Mr. Hawthorne, should be followed by two others who were devoting their lives to young people. My mother, under the pen name "Margaret Sidney," had already written *The Five Little Peppers and How They Grew*. My father was often referred to as "The Children's Publisher."

Daniel Lothrop had founded his publishing firm, D. Lothrop & Co., in 1868. A great reader from childhood, he early became interested in developing for young people a literature adapted to their needs. This purpose could best be accomplished, he believed, through a careful study of children's vocabularies at different ages and of the parallel intellectual interests. He realized that nature, when it was accurately and entertainingly described, offered a special field for children's books. In search of experts in certain branches of science, he appealed to various university professors. At first they were indignant at the thought of writing for children, but it was not long before many recognized the importance and challenge of the project.

Among other problems was the question of illustrations. Here again he believed that experts should be employed; Childe Hassam is only one of the many fine artists whose pictures were published in *Wide Awake,* one of the four Lothrop magazines for young people. *Little Men and Women, Our Pansy,* and *Babyland*—the other three—were all popular, but the most important was *Wide Awake,* which was designed for the older children. In it appeared poems, stories, and articles of general interest written by men and women who have taken high rank in the literature of the country. Louise Imogen Guiney, Elizabeth Stuart Phelps, Mary E. Wilkins, Sarah Orne Jewett, Celia Thaxter, and Edward Everett Hale are only a few of the authors who contributed to the magazine. Although Mr. Lothrop published many fine books for adults, his leadership in developing a literature for young people was recognized.

Dr. Edward Everett Hale has written of my father: "An American through and through, he represents American Education at its best." In addition to his other standards for children's stories, Mr. Lothrop believed that they should avoid sentimentality and should attempt to portray natural children under homelike surroundings. In summing up his characteristics as a publisher, Dr. Hale quoted two of Mr. Lothrop's own phrases: [1]

---

[1] Edward Everett Hale, "An American Publisher," *Lend a Hand,* IX, 263 (October, 1892).

1. Never to publish a book purely sensational, no matter what the chances of money it has in it.

2. To publish books which will make for true, steadfast growth in right living.

To a publisher with such ideals, it was a pleasure to read in his own magazine in 1880 about the adventures of a courageous and natural family group, the Five Little Peppers. He was surprised to find that very small children could be made to appear on paper as if they were wholly alive. He became interested in this new family and wondered what their author, "Margaret Sidney," might be like. Since he was soon going to New York on business, he decided to stop in New Haven and call on her. When my mother used to tell about this visit, she would keep her face quite straight, without a smile, and say: "He seemed to have business in New York again in two weeks, and a little unfinished in New Haven—and again in two weeks." As a smile crept around her mouth, and her blue eyes began to dance, she added simply, "And then the New *York* business did not seem so important!"

"Margaret Sidney" was really Miss Harriett Mulford Stone, the daughter of the architect Sidney Mason Stone of New Haven, Connecticut. He was well known, partly because he had designed many churches and institutional buildings, and partly because he had collected around him a group of brilliant and devoted students. My aunt tells me that for a number of years before the establishment of its own department Yale College had sent young men who were interested in architecture to Mr. Stone for instruction in his offices on Chapel Street just above Orange. Well to do and dignified, a "gentleman of the old school," my grandfather looked with disfavor upon young women who wrote for publication. When his progressive daughter found that her verse and short stories were being accepted by magazines, she considered the question of a pen name, having hitherto used her own initials, H.M.S. She did not wish to bring opprobrium upon her father's name, nor did she wish wholly to desert it, since she dearly loved him. The following notation about her pen name was found among her papers and would seem to have been written in answer to some questions by a newspaper or magazine interviewer:

> I chose my penname "Sidney" because it was my father's first name. He was a splendid man, strong and true, & that made me like "Sidney" which I had always liked from "Sir Philip" down. Besides I wanted something a good deal different from the lackadaisical soubriquets that were frequently selected in the "seventies," when I chose mine. "Margaret" was my favorite name for a girl *not* because it means "Pearl" and "Daisy" but because it means *Truth*. So there you have it—Truth and justice or chivalry, or

whatever you call the broad helpful influence diffused by "Sidney."

I chose to write under a penname just as thousands of others do I suppose. I was not going to be good game for derision if I failed.

She went on to say that while she was serving her apprenticeship at writing she had no intention of disturbing her family's peace of mind by calling attention to the fledgling author in their midst.

"Margaret Sidney" and her publisher, Daniel Lothrop, were married on October 4, 1881. Until the spring of 1883 they boarded, either in Boston or in Cambridge, but like the Alcotts and Hawthornes, they, too, wished to have their own home. When they came to The Wayside, my father was fifty-one years of age, a man of medium height, about five feet nine inches. His portly build, gray hair and beard might have made him look settled had it not been for his erect carriage and the unusually direct gaze of his blue eyes. His quick sympathetic understanding and clear-cut reasoning made conversation with him memorable. Mother was nearly thirty-nine. Her blue eyes, regular features, and naturally pink cheeks were framed by brown hair in which twinkled red gold lights. A woman of enthusiasm, charm, and graciousness, she had worked out a philosophy of action based upon a strong religious faith. The following statement so truly portrays many of her ideals as I knew them, that I believe it to be original with her. Although not signed, it is in her handwriting and was found among her manuscripts.

PROMISE YOURSELF

To be so strong that nothing can disturb your peace of mind.

To talk of health, happiness and prosperity to every person you meet.

To make all your friends feel that there is something to them.

To look on the sunny side of everything and make your optimism come true.

To think only of the best, to work only for the best, and to expect only the best.

To be just as enthusiastic about [the] success of others as you are about your own.

To forget the mistakes of the past and press on to the greater achievements of the future.

To wear a cheerful countenance at all times, and to have a smile ready for [every] living creature you meet.

To give so much time to the improvement of yourself that you have no time to criticise others.

To be too large for worry, too noble for anger, too strong for fear, and too happy to permit the presence of trouble.

To think well of yourself and to proclaim this fact to the world —not in loud words, but in great deeds.

To live to the faith that the world is on your side so long as you are true to the best that is in you.

A keen sense of duty was added to this cheerful and courageous attitude towards life. Work came before play, but fortunately work was to her a real joy. I have watched her many times when she was busily writing a book. She would lean slightly on her left elbow, and with head somewhat bent, watch her pen as it moved over the paper. Generally a light of inner happiness was on her face; if she happened to see me, she would look up and smile, then turn back, with determination but with evident contentment to her writing.

Like my father she, too, was a pioneer in her work for children and in her attitude towards them. She was able to understand the individual child, his impulses and re-actions, the way his mind worked. I have heard her tell a story to a group of children, unfolding her narrative simply, yet with the detail they demanded; and I have at the same time watched the children as they listened, hardly breathing in the intensity of their interest. There was nothing careless or accidental about her repetition of details, nor about the slow movement of her scenes. She was one of the first authors to base her writing upon this psychological understanding, both of the little children in her books and of her child readers or listeners.

She and Father showed their interest in children in other ways than in the writing or publishing of books and magazines. They both felt that young people, as future citizens, should have an opportunity to learn intimately of the ideals and courageous actions of those who struggled for liberty during the early days of our country. Mother has written that she and Father had often discussed the necessity for a patriotic society for young people, which should be based on the principles of the Constitution. They both realized that organizations for adults could not be adapted to this need, but that young people should have their own meetings, suited to their own requirements, and quite separate from those of adults. Several years after Father's death, the ideas they had discussed were to take shape in the Children of the American Revolution, a national society organized by my mother in 1895.

Closely connected with this intelligent patriotism was their respect for the memorials of the past and their desire to preserve them. As has been mentioned, this desire influenced them greatly when they bought The Wayside and decided to change the old house as little as possible. The superficial nature of the few repairs which from time to time they found to be necessary indicates the constant care which was exercised. The woodwork of the two lower front rooms had been painted a dull gray after the Hawthornes had left the house; it was now changed to more cheerful colors. For the dining room a soft terra cotta was chosen, and for the sitting room a warm dark green which contrasted pleasantly with a light ecru cartridge paper. The Hawthorne paint and wallpaper, however, were retained far beyond their natural life. In later years when it became imperative to replace the front hall paper, my mother searched the shops to secure the same color and general pattern.

Yet for all their great respect for the past, my parents were not slavish in their devotion. They believed that a home should be comfortable, and that it should be adapted to the needs of the family occupying it, providing such adaptations involved no fundamental changes. Father installed a furnace, for example, when they decided to remain at The Wayside through the late fall and Christmas seasons. Generally they spent the winters in a hotel in Boston, to be near my father's office. For comfort in hot weather a wide piazza was added to the western wing, making a large outdoor sitting room, reached by two long doorways leading from Mr. Hawthorne's old library.

At a much later date the fireplace in the "Old Room," or what had been the Alcott's kitchen, became unsafe. When Mother was obliged to rebuild this section of the central chimney, she had the angle of the hearth somewhat altered so that a group might more comfortably sit in front of it. However, she retained old English bricks which the workmen found built into the chimney, and she rehung the old iron door of the oven. I have often heard her explain to friends that the new oven was built to "the exact measurements of the old one."

My mother took keen interest in all details of the
early construction of The Wayside, and was especially
pleased when certain discoveries were made in 1907. In
that year she decided that the room that had been Mrs.
Hawthorne's parlor was not sufficiently easy of access,
since it could be reached only through the long front hall.
She determined, therefore, to cut through the partition
separating the parlor and the colonial sitting room. The
solid construction of the wall surprised us all, but particularly the carpenter, whose expression became more
and more puzzled as his saw almost refused to move.
When he finally succeeded in making an opening, we dis-

Fireplace in the "Old Room." About 1900

covered that the wall of the sitting room, formerly the northern outside wall of the colonial house, consisted of four layers: modern plaster, old plaster, handmade bricks, and old shingles. Built directly against these shingles was the wall of the parlor, making in all a partition fourteen inches thick. The discovery of the handmade clay bricks interested Mother as an example of the ingenuity of the colonial builders, who were determined to protect themselves from the cold north winds.

My parents had nine summers at The Wayside before my father's death in 1892. I was only a small girl of seven when he died, but I remember clearly their happiness and companionship. One recollection is of their evening conferences about literary matters. I was too young, of course, to stay up or enter into the consultations, but I knew that he and Mother often contentedly spent several hours discussing manuscripts or other publishing problems after I had been put to bed.

Both my mother and father were fond of good conversation and music, and enjoyed welcoming friends to our home. A cousin, slightly older than I, was visiting us when I was four years old. She clearly remembers that guests were almost always present at our dinner table. Among her other memories of the summer she spent with us is an amusing one about a musicale which Mother gave. We had at that time a huge St. Bernard dog whose name, if I remember correctly, was Sancho

Panza. I am sure that he was huge because I could barely reach high enough to put my arm over his neck. Like many other dogs he had a great dislike for music, especially singing. For that reason precautions had been taken and he had been tied in the barn. In some way he had broken loose and entered the music room, stalking up behind the unsuspecting singer, who was accompanying herself at the piano. With no warning, and before anyone in the audience could move, first one of his enormous paws and then the other hit the keyboard. He then put back his head and gave an unearthly howl.

Mother, with her ready wit, was equal to any occasion. I have no doubt that, by some humorous remark, she added to her guests' enjoyment of this unexpected contribution to her program. Such incidents would increase her fund of anecdotes, a fund which seemed inexhaustible. Always amusing, she was at her best when narrating stories at her own expense.

I know that Mother enjoyed giving large entertainments, but, as I have already said, I was only seven when Father died, and I therefore do not remember details of the receptions she gave during those years. I do recall that the guests filled the house and overflowed to the lawn. At the foot of the stone wall, just under the slope of the hill, tables were set for serving ice cream and punch, the green spruce trees above the gray wall making the colors of the ladies' dresses seem particularly gay.

Much more clear in my mind are the memories of the large birthday fetes which my mother and father gave for me. Mother would write a poem for the celebration and arrange a special entertainment, in which a number of my little friends would take part. On my fourth birthday a group of little girls came dancing down the hillside and around the lawn. My cousin tells me that she was one of this group and distinctly remembers how Miss Elizabeth Palmer Peabody taught them the steps they were to take, and, on the occasion itself, gave them a little speech. The dancers, like so many butterflies, circled around an enormous artificial rose. I was the little girl supposed to be called from the opening rosebud by their beckonings and pleadings. I am afraid that at the moment, I did not appreciate all of Mother's efforts on my behalf. Too vividly etched on my memory is the impatience I felt for the cue which would free me from my hot prison.

More enjoyable, from my point of view, was my fifth birthday party, in which Miss Ellen Emerson, the daughter of the philosopher, was mistress of ceremonies. Rain had driven us into the barn for the entertainment. I remember marching through four flower-decorated arches, at each of which I was given a white rose. At the fifth arch a crown of white roses was placed on my head, after which we all joined in the dances and childhood games, led by Miss Ellen, as we affectionately called her.

As I look back now after all these years, I am glad that I can remember her dancing with us little children in the same barn in which she, in her own childhood, some forty years earlier, had been taught by Louisa Alcott.

Although my early memories are naturally limited, I also remember certain quiet evenings at home when friends were visiting us and when I was allowed to sit up beyond my usual bedtime. Curled up in Mr. Hawthorne's comfortable red leather armchair, I would drift off to sleep, with the odor of Father's Havana cigar and the gentle flow of voices my last memory.

One of my father's special friends was John Greenleaf Whittier, to whose home I was taken on many occasions when I was five or six years old. To me he was not the famous poet, but one of my very best friends whom I dearly loved. He seemed to talk to me without words, and I remember the feeling of real companionship with him. Mother, in her book, *Whittier with the Children*, written within a year of his death, said that I used to call him, "My very dear Mr. Whittier." My own memory has retained only two scenes, but they are clear: once when he was digging violets for me at his own home, and the other time when he held me on his lap and told me stories. This last scene stands out with especial distinctness because a jealous little black-and-tan dog snapped at my ankles. I lifted my ankles up as far as possible from the attack, while Mr. Whittier gently held me with his left arm,—reassuring me at the same time,—and just as gently pushed away the snapping dog with his right hand. I never remember him when he was not singularly gentle. His warm, rich voice gave a tenderness to his usual quiet greeting, "How *is* thee, Margaret?"

Among other of my early recollections was my father's devotion to Mr. Whittier's poetry. Father could repeat without hesitation many of the longer poems. Once, at an evening meeting in the chapel of the Old South Church in Boston, the pastor, Dr. George A. Gordon, stated that a friend in the congregation knew by heart the not too familiar "Andrew Rykman's Prayer." Dr. Gordon hoped that his friend, who had not been warned of the request, would be willing to repeat the lines which were particularly appropriate to the subject of the meeting. I am told that Father, without a moment's hesitation, and without moving from his seat, recited the complete poem.

This devotion to Mr. Whittier's poetry was no new interest with Father, as was shown by the well-worn copy of the poems of the Quaker poet, which he gave to Mother apparently about the time of their engagement. Many markers are still between the leaves, and on the flyleaf, in Father's handwriting, is the name, "Miss Hattie M. Stone," and the date, "August 1st, 1881." Beneath, in Mr. Whittier's handwriting, is the following verse, now published for the first time.

No author loves to see his books
Kept always fresh and new;
This well-worn volume really looks
As if well read by you.
As if you found the grain of grace
And truth beneath its commonplace;
Discerned the half-expressed intent
And guessed aright the good I meant.
So owning all its fault and lack
I send it to the Wayside back.

John G. Whittier

Dec. 24, 1891

Another author who was a friend of my parents as well as of the Hawthornes was Dr. Oliver Wendell Holmes. He, too, was kind to me. Once when I was about ten years old, Mother took me to call on him at his country home at Beverly Farms, on the occasion of his eighty-fifth birthday. At the end of the visit he wanted to give me a copy of a small paper-covered edition of *Selections* from his writings. We hunted together through his tall glass-fronted bookcases, and at last found a copy in a lower drawer. Dr. Holmes went to a small desk, and not bothering with a chair, knelt in front of it while he wrote. Childlike I put my arm over his shoulder and watched him write my name and his name. When he had finished, he looked up into my face, not far from his. His own face broke into that winning smile of his, as he said, "Well, Margaret, pretty good for an old boy, isn't it?"

My father's death occurred in 1892. For the next two years my mother undertook the management of the publishing firm until its sale to three young men, former employees of my father. At the time of the sale the firm's name was changed to Lothrop Publishing Company. In 1904 that firm was combined with another well-known Boston publishing house, under the present name, Lothrop, Lee and Shepard.

Released from these business responsibilities, Mother returned to her literary work with redoubled vigor. After her marriage she had written two books describing the further adventures of the Pepper family: *Five Little Peppers Midway* and *Five Little Peppers Grown Up*. Many other stories had come from her pen, New England tales for adults, as well as stories for children. Her favorite characters, however, were the imaginary Pepper children, Ben, Polly, Joel, Davie, and Phronsie.

From her early girlhood, Mother had delighted in creating imaginary people. She has often told me that even when very young, she "just had to write," scribbling and tearing up the stories, then writing and destroying again and again, until she was fairly well satisfied with the results.

The following reminiscences of her childhood I

found recently among her papers. It is a rough draft, perhaps preliminary jottings for some preface.

DATA ABOUT MY WRITING THE PEPPERS

One of the first things that I call from my childish book of remembrance is that I played with the children of my imagination. I had "lots" (as the children say) of girl and boy friends, and I was an out-of-door little creature as far as restricted city life would allow. But I dearly loved to get away and curled up in a big chair in the Library, or under a large table where the ample cloth fell down and successfully hid me from the children "tagging" me, then it was that I peopled my world with all sorts of playmates that real life did not afford. . . .

Well, it is impossible to say when the "Peppers" really began. At any rate, when [as] a slip of a girl I would be taken to ride in the country I always longed to find a little brown house, well settled down at the back, and a good bit from the road. I knew exactly how the little path ran up to the big green door, and the grass tried to grow in the front yard. And around it all was the glorious expanse of real country fields. Oh, how I longed for that to be my home. I could not understand how my father who was a most successful architect, ever had been so foolish as to live in a big city and not in this place, where I might have hens and chickens, and scratch the back of the pigs. A little girl friend had once harrowed my very soul by telling me of that bliss once when she spent a day in the country, and I couldn't speak to her for a week without tears of envy and vexation.

Then as I couldn't find the counterpart of my little brown house, I said "I will make one for myself." So that began "the little brown house in Badgertown" that all children love.

Mother went on to say that of course there must be children in the house. She liked boys and they liked her, so she decided to give the preponderance to them in the Pepper family, three boys and two girls. Without realizing it she must have written of herself in Polly, for in this thoughtful, independent little girl I find a great deal of Mother as she must have been at the same age. Cheerful courage and the wish to make other people happy were in both the imaginary Polly Pepper and her author-creator. How Mother was able to depict impoverished country life, so different from her own, has always amazed me. In describing the Pepper family, Mother continued in her informal reminiscences:

Then there was Mrs. Pepper. *Unconsciously* I put into her character some of my mother's qualities. Unconsciously I say, for I never copied any one, nor any sayings of people in my stories.

Now my judgment told me that I must eliminate Mr. Pepper, because the whole *motif* "to help Mother" would be lost, if the father lived. It hurt me dreadfully. He was a most estimable man, and I loved my own father so much, it seemed the most wicked thing to do. I went around for days, feeling droopy and guilty. But it had to be done. . . .

Well all the above came on gradually, as I thought and played with the Peppers. . . I never had an idea of printing my brain children. It was one thing to "yarn" to the other children . . . but quite another to realize that anybody really wanted to know them. So the years passed, and I passed along with them, thinking and writing, and having awfully good times with all the creatures of my imagination, till, and I was as much surprised as any one, they simply had to get between book covers. It was this way: I sent one of the Pepper "yarns" to the Wide Awake. It was "Polly Pepper's Chicken Pie"—This was followed by "Phronsie Pepper's New Shoes"—The Editor wrote asking me to fill out a year with Pepper Stories. . . .

In these words I can hear my mother speaking. Whenever she used to tell friends about the origin of the Pepper books, and reached this point in her recital, she would always stop, and hesitate, as if she could still remember her fear that she might not have enough to say to fill out a twelve-months' serial. Then her blue eyes would twinkle, as they so often did, and she would add that ultimately she had written twelve books about these same children!

The Peppers became as real to me when I was a little girl, as they were to Mother, although I did not have a creative imagination, and was therefore obliged to wait for a new book, in order to learn about their latest adventures. I realized that Mother, however, seemed to commune with them when she was writing a book. When I was a young girl, she and I would often sit in front of the open fire in the old sitting room. She would be rocking in her comfortable brown wicker chair, and I, wanting to read yet hesitating to do so for fear she might be lonely, would ask her if I couldn't bring her a book and a lamp. She would say, "No"; then seeing my hesitancy, would turn with that charming smile of hers, and reassure me. "Oh, no, Margaret. I am happy; I am just thinking of the Peppers." Quietly she would continue her rocking and I, content, would open my book. Once in a while I would look up to see how she was, and often I would catch a little smile stealing across her face, just as if she were listening to an amusing story being told her by someone I could not see—one of the Pepper children, I knew.

I could almost see them clustered around Mother

and her chair, they seemed so real to me. The mental picture is as vivid today as it was then. Polly, dark eyes dancing, and brown hair encircling her eager face, stood close against Mother's right elbow. Phronsie, with the golden hair, leaned on Mother's right knee, gazing into her face—I knew that expression of earnest interest. Sturdy old Ben hung over the back of the chair, while Davie, almost breathless with excitement, stood a little way off. Joel was jumping up and down with eagerness; he would joggle Mother's left arm and I felt I could hear him say, his dark head nodding to give his words the proper emphasis: "You haven't heard about this!"

The Lothrop Sitting Room at The Wayside

As Mother has written, and as she has often said to friends, the Peppers were entirely imaginary. They were so real to her, however, that when she was asked why she made them do this or that—for instance, why she made Joel fall out of the apple tree and break his arm—she would answer, "*I* make them!" Her blue eyes would open wide as she continued: "I didn't make them do anything. They did what they wanted to do; then came and told me about it, and I just wrote it down!" Nevertheless, the cheerful acceptance of difficulties and the search for joy in everyday life by the Pepper family were not chance occurrences. They were inner attributes of my mother; she could no more have helped expressing them than she could have helped breathing. When grief and financial difficulties did come to her with my father's death, she met them as courageously and as cheerfully as did the Peppers any of their problems.

In the introductions to the later volumes she has written of the visits which the Peppers made to The Wayside to tell her of their adventures. In one introduction, that for *Our Davie*, she mentions visiting Badgertown. Many persons have asked Mother whether there was a real town of that name. She answered that she had no town in mind, and that Badgertown, like the Little Brown House, was the product of her imagination. She went on to say that she did not at first think of the children as the *Pepper* family, but as Phronsie or Joel;

that is, as individuals. When it became necessary to give them a surname, she was in a quandary. As she has so often stated, she never consciously described an individual nor repeated actual conversations. In fact, I have often heard her make strongly derogatory remarks about certain authors who had, in their books, infringed upon the personalities of individuals to such an extent that these individuals could be recognized. In addition to not describing actual persons, Mother tried to avoid giving an unpleasant character a name which might belong to an innocent, kindly disposed person. In spite of her efforts, the following incident had occurred just a short time before she was faced with the necessity of naming her new book family. In one of her stories she had introduced a thoroughly disagreeable, crotchety New Englander and had taken pains to choose an unlikely name. She had turned to the Bible for the first name, Jeroboam, if I remember correctly. The surname was also unusual. Almost immediately after the publication of the story, a letter arrived from an irate woman who wanted to know how "Margaret Sidney" had heard of her father, and why she had so exactly described him!

With this experience fresh in her mind Mother determined to find a name which no one possessed. As she did not wish one which would be difficult to remember, she decided to choose the word for some well-known object. One day, as she sat at her father's dinner table, the solution flashed into her mind. In front of her were salt and pepper. "Splendid," she thought, "everyone knows these words, yet no one is named Salt or Pepper." When my mother told this story, she would wrinkle up her nose, as if she were displeased. "Mary Salt. Joe Salt." Her smile danced again. "Mary Pepper,—oh, *Polly* Pepper. Joe Pepper,—*Joel* Pepper. *Phronsie* Pepper! And so they were named Pepper." She often laughed over the joke on her, when, years afterward, a family named Pepper moved to Concord, built their home near The Wayside, and became her good friends.

The care with which Mother chose the name for the Pepper family is illustrative of her serious, although affectionate, attitude towards her literary work. When she was in the midst of writing, all social entertainment of any formal kind was put aside until the book or article was completed. Yet I never felt that she regarded her work as an onerous task, but rather it was something to which she wanted to give her best powers. It was as if an inner force, greater than herself, urged her on to a labor which filled her with joy, even while it took her away from the social life which at other times gave her great pleasure. When a book was being written, my mother devoted about eight hours a day to it, from six to eight and from ten to twelve in the morning and from one to five in the afternoon. Such hours meant hard physical work as well as mental labor, because every word was in long hand. She never wrote in the evening, but sat in front of the fire, rocking and thinking, or perhaps reading. Only when proof arrived, did she give any sign of annoyance in connection with her writing.

Many times I have been asked whether Mother told me stories. Indeed she did, and generously, provided I asked for them at a sensible time! When she had agreed, she would sit quietly, hands in her lap and head slightly bent, for about half a minute. Then she would straighten up and smilingly begin. The story would wind on and on, always holding my keen attention—I would have hated to miss a single word—until a logical ending was reached. To this day I have never been able to understand how, in the short time she allowed herself before starting, she could have evolved a complicated plot which *always* had logic in its conclusion, whether that was sad or happy.

As far as I can remember, Mother's stories to me were never about the Pepper children. I expected to learn of their adventures from her books, awaiting the advent of each new volume with the suppressed excitement of any other young girl. My particular advantage was that Mother—after Father's death—always wrote my name in the first copy she touched. When the box of new books arrived from the publishers, and the cover had been removed, Mother would pick up a copy, glance at the illustrations, read a bit here and there, and always write my name on the flyleaf. Then I would waste no further time until I had read that book.

The manuscript of a story complete and the disagreeable task of correcting proof finished, Mother would resume her interrupted social life. I remember the afternoons when the East Quarter Reading Circle, which had been started by Miss Ellen Emerson, came to The Wayside. For several years it met more or less regularly at various homes in this section of town. On one particular day I had listened to the ladies gathered in our dining room discussing whether or not they should begin before Miss Ellen arrived. Shortly afterward I happened to glance out of the window in time to see Miss Ellen riding her bicycle past the house. I was surprised that she had not entered, and my surprise grew with the passing moments. Finally she arrived, out of breath, explaining that she had been obliged to ride some distance past our house before she found a man to stop her bicycle and help her dismount. Miss Ellen was never one to be deterred by what she considered trivial matters. That she was just recovering from a severe case of water on the knee did not discourage her from using her bicycle, even though she could not mount or dismount without help. There was always, as she explained, some man or boy about who could help her. In earlier years mounted on her little gray donkey, predecessor to the bicycle, her feet barely escaping the ground, Miss Ellen was a familiar figure on the sidewalks in Concord, as beloved as she was individual.

Fond as Mother was of informal gatherings such as the East Quarter Reading Circle, she entered with zest into the planning of large entertainments and thoroughly enjoyed every moment of a fete while it was in progress. I remember with what pleasure she arranged the details of a literary afternoon at The Wayside in honor of Frank B. Sanborn, our townsman, and with what care she made plans for another large meeting held in memory of Mr. Ephraim Wales Bull, the originator of the Concord grape.

Probably the most important gathering of this period was the celebration in 1904 of the Hawthorne centenary. It lasted for four days and was largely attended. Papers were read by men and women who had known Hawthorne; Rose Hawthorne Lathrop, then Mother Mary Alphonsa, and her brother, Julian Hawthorne, sent letters. A boulder was unveiled by a granddaughter Beatrix Hawthorne to mark the author's favorite path to his hilltop. Receptions interspersed the numerous literary meetings.

On one of the afternoons I recall coming across a very special little group in a corner of the sitting room, the sun shining on their four white heads, which were close together. All four had known Mr. Hawthorne, and had written about him. They were Mrs. Julia Ward

Howe, Colonel Thomas Wentworth Higginson, Mr. Moncure Conway, and Mr. Frank B. Sanborn. I could hear a softly spoken "Do you remember . . . ?" followed by a peal of laughter. Perhaps among the tales Mr. Sanborn may have reminded them of his adventure in The Wayside many years before, where he had been hidden following the capture, at Harpers Ferry, of his friend, John Brown. In 1860 it had been no laughing matter!

Interested as my mother was in the social and literary life of her friends and acquaintances, she never forgot that her vocation and her most joyous companionship was with children. Busy as she might be at some par-

Boulder at Foot of Hawthorne's Path.   Unveiled in 1904

ticular moment, she was ever aware of their presence. She felt, as she once explained, that there were no barriers, but that she and they spoke the same language.

The right of children to a joyous life she expressed in her books; and their right to pride in the achievements of their ancestors was just as significant to her. For her, patriotism combined pride in the past, love of country, an understanding of its best traditions, and a will to translate all of those values and traditions into the life of the present. The adults had their own organizations, the Daughters of the American Revolution and the Sons of the American Revolution. However, these organizations did not admit minors. She, therefore, interested some of her friends and organized the National Society, Children of the American Revolution. It was a fitting memorial to my father, who had discussed with her its possibility. To the first meeting, held in Washington in 1895, were invited parents and children who might be interested in such a project, and at that meeting the first members were enrolled. As national president Mother gave freely of her time and energy during the first difficult years of development. The Old North Bridge Society of Concord was the first local organization, and had many of its early meetings at The Wayside. Today the National Society C.A.R., still flourishing, provides an opportunity for young people to learn the achievements of the founders of our republic and to understand the vision that inspired them. During the present period of national uncertainty, it is a valuable force working for sane patriotism and democratic ideals.

It was largely for the sake of young people that my mother exerted herself to the utmost to save houses of historic interest. She realized that with the passing of time, old houses rich in associations might be destroyed or irremediably changed. When, in 1902, the Orchard House property was to be sold, she determined that the home where Louisa Alcott had done so much of her writing should be preserved for the young people of the future. She therefore bought it and held it for ten years, until the Louisa May Alcott Memorial Association was formed for its preservation and maintenance.

Likewise, when Mr. Ephraim Wales Bull died, she bought his old home. Its need of repair was so great that partial rebuilding was necessary. Yet she kept the beauty and charm of his little cottage. Another old house in whose preservation she took an active part is situated opposite Wright Tavern, in the very center of Concord, where Lexington Road joins the Milldam. It was proposed to tear down the house and to erect on its site a new and large structure. Realizing that a fine old landmark should not be lost, Mother consulted with friends and also with the Old Concord Chapter of the Daughters of the American Revolution of which she had been the founder and first Regent. A fund was raised which made it possible for the Concord Chapter to purchase and preserve this house which so greatly contributed to Concord's old-time beauty.

As the years had passed, books had continued to come from Mother's pen, in all some thirty or forty; the series about the Five Little Peppers had grown to twelve volumes; there had been other favorites, such as *The Little Maid of Concord Town* and its companion volume about Boston. She had remembered her birthplace, New Haven, Connecticut, in *The Judge's Cave, a Romance of the*

Home of Ephraim Wales Bull with the Original Concord Grape Vine. About 1895

Regicides. Perhaps even more interesting was the chatty semi-guidebook, *Old Concord: Her Highways and By-ways.*

In her later years Mother spent a good deal of time in travel, taking trips of some duration to Egypt and Palestine as well as to England, Norway, and the Continent. She found particular joy in such out-of-the-way spots as Spitzbergen and in places with literary associations. The last nine winters of her life she spent in California where she had many friends and where she could work with greater ease than in the more rigorous climate of New England. The breadth of the continent, however, did not separate her spirit from Concord and the home which was filled for her with associations.

Nor did she ever lose her love of writing; shortly before her death August 2, 1924, at the age of eighty, she completed an article on Edgar Allan Poe, in connection with a proposal to name a square in his honor. Her mind was so active and she found life so interesting up to the very end that, as she had said many years earlier, she "just had to write."

At the time of my mother's death and for several years afterwards, The Wayside was rented to tenants not belonging to either the Hawthorne or Lothrop families. When these tenants moved from Concord, the question of the future of the house had to be faced. I disliked the thought of selling it to a private family, who might not feel the obligation towards its past and towards the public which my father and mother had from the first so clearly recognized. The house had acquired an individuality of its own, derived partly from its multiple roofs but partly also perhaps from a less tangible debt to its author-owners. In it was still much of the Hawthorne and practically all of the Lothrop furniture. It was therefore opened to the public in 1927, at first during my absence under a committee and later under my own direction.

Not until the hurricane of September, 1938, was there any destruction of The Wayside property. Unfortunately at that time the lovely spruce trees, grown to a height of eighty feet, were snapped off or uprooted. Their beauty cannot be replaced within our generation. More important is the loss of the literary associations of these particular trees. When little saplings, nearly eighty years ago, they had been sent from abroad by Mr. Hawthorne and planted on the terraces which Mr. Alcott had so laboriously cut in the steep hillside.

Sometimes now, when I look at the bare terraces behind the house, the destruction of those towering trees seems almost unendurable. They had not only formed a dark-green frame for The Wayside, but they had also created a shaded, sun-flecked retreat. Then I catch myself reflecting that the sunshine which now floods Mrs. Hawthorne's parlor has changed it from the gloomy place I had always known to the cheerful room Mrs.

Hawthorne must have had when the trees were tiny. With their loss and with the thinning of trees on the farther slope of the hill, the wide vista over the meadows, so dearly loved by Mr. Hawthorne, is once more visible from his hilltop path where he used to pace back and forth as he planned his future work.

Even more thankfully I remember that the house itself was not damaged by the hurricane. Within it one can still easily picture Mr. Hawthorne reading aloud to his family; Louisa and her sisters acting out their plays or listening to their father's gentle teaching; and the Five Little Peppers crowding around their author-creator.

It is my hope that the old house may never become merely a museum, but rather that it may remain as it is today with its home life of the past still about it. The Wayside, as long as it is unchanged, has much to tell those who, with the ears and the eyes of imagination, can hear the murmurs of the pines and spruces on the terraces, the sound of children at play, and the gentle voices of its honored authors.

Chronologies

CHRONOLOGY OF THE THREE FAMILIES OF AUTHORS

Amos Bronson Alcott
> born November 29, 1799 in Wolcott, Connecticut
> married May 23, 1830 in Boston to Abigail May, daughter of Colonel Joseph May
> died March 4, 1888 in Boston

Abigail (May) Alcott
> born October 8, 1800 in Boston
> died November 25, 1877 in Concord, Massachusetts

THEIR CHILDREN

> Anna Bronson
>> born March 16, 1831 in Germantown, Pennsylvania
>> married May 23, 1860 in Concord to John Pratt of Concord
>> died July 17, 1893 in Concord

> Louisa May
>> born November 29, 1832 in Germantown, Pennsylvania
>> died March 6, 1888 in Roxbury, Massachusetts

Elizabeth Sewall
  born June 24, 1835 in Boston
  died March 14, 1858 in Concord

Abba May
  born July 28, 1840 in Concord
  married March 22, 1878 in London, England to
    Ernest Niericker
  died December 29, 1879 in Paris, France

Nathaniel Hawthorne
  born July 4, 1804 in Salem, Massachusetts
  married July 9, 1842 in Boston to Sophia Amelia Pea-
    body, daughter of Dr. Nathaniel Peabody
  died May 19, 1864 in Plymouth, New Hampshire

Sophia Amelia (Peabody) Hawthorne
  born September 21, 1809 in Salem, Massachusetts
  died February 26, 1871 in London, England

  THEIR CHILDREN
    Una
      born March 3, 1844 in Concord
      died September 10, 1877 in Clewer, England
    Julian
      born June 22, 1846 in Boston
      married November 15, 1870 to Mary Albertina
        Amelung in New York, New York
      married (2d 1925) to Edith Garrigues
      died July 14, 1934 in San Francisco

Rose
> born May 20, 1851 in Lenox, Massachusetts
> married September 11, 1871 to George Parsons Lathrop
> became Mother Mary Alphonsa December 8, 1900
> died July 9, 1926 at Rosary Hill Home in Hawthorne, New York

Daniel Lothrop
> born August 11, 1831 in Rochester, New Hampshire
> married October 4, 1881 in New Haven, Connecticut to Harriett Mulford Stone, daughter of Sidney Mason Stone
> died March 18, 1892 in Boston

Harriett Mulford (Stone) Lothrop
> born June 22, 1844 in New Haven, Connecticut
> died August 2, 1924 in San Francisco

Eleven authors—if we include those who have published one book—have made their home in The Wayside either as children or as adults; some have lived in the house at several periods of their lives. By birth or marriage all were connected with three families.

THE ALCOTTS
> Mr. Amos Bronson Alcott
> Miss Louisa May Alcott
> Miss Abba May Alcott (Mrs. Ernest Niericker)

THE HAWTHORNES

Mr. Nathaniel Hawthorne

Mrs. Nathaniel Hawthorne (Sophia Peabody)

Mr. Julian Hawthorne

Mrs. Rose Hawthorne Lathrop (Mrs. George Parsons Lathrop)

Mr. George Parsons Lathrop

Mrs. Horace Mann (Mary Peabody)

Miss Hildegarde Hawthorne (Mrs. Oskison), a daughter of Julian Hawthorne

MRS. DANIEL LOTHROP ("MARGARET SIDNEY")

The name of Miss Elizabeth Palmer Peabody is not included in this list because it is not known that she made The Wayside her home for a definite period of time as did the others. Yet she should be mentioned, since she frequently visited her sisters, Mrs. Hawthorne and Mrs. Mann, and their brother, Dr. Nathaniel Peabody during their periods of residence at The Wayside. While the Hawthornes were abroad, The Wayside was occupied first by Dr. Peabody and his family, and later by Mrs. Mann and her three sons. In still later years Miss Peabody visited Mr. and Mrs. Daniel Lothrop. Miss Peabody is distinctly a part of The Wayside history.

CHRONOLOGY OF THE PROPERTY

1666

Nathaniel Ball, Sr. recorded ownership of a "house lott" of 13 acres.

1688

Nathaniel Ball, Sr. deeded to his son, Nathaniel Ball, Jr., the unimproved half of the "house lott," the other half to go to Nathaniel, Jr. on the death of the father.

1717

Caleb Ball, son of Nathaniel, Jr., sold his house and barn with 3¾ acres, plus other farming land.

1717–1769

The house was owned and occupied by Samuel Fletcher, Jr., Nathaniel Colburn, and John Breede.

1769–1778

Owned by Samuel Whitney, who occupied it until 1776.

1778–1827

Owned and occupied by Daniel Hoar, Sr. and by his son, Daniel, Jr., until the latter's death in 1823. Daniel, Jr.'s heirs sold it in 1827, some of them occupying the house between 1823 and 1827.

1827–1832

Owned by Darius Merriam, who lived in it most of those years.

1832–1845

Owned by Horatio Cogswell, who made it his home during some of that time. In 1836 the house was occupied by Albert Lawrence Bull, brother of Ephraim Wales Bull.

1845–1852

Owned by trustees for Mrs. Amos Bronson Alcott. The house was the home of Mr. and Mrs. Alcott and their four daughters, from April 1, 1845 to November 17, 1848.

1852–1870
>Owned by Nathaniel Hawthorne and his heirs and occupied:
>>1852–1853 by Mr. Hawthorne and his family until they went abroad.
>>1853–1859 by Mrs. Hawthorne's brother, Dr. Nathaniel Peabody, and his family.
>>1859–1860 by Mrs. Hawthorne's sister, Mrs. Horace Mann, and her three sons after the death of Mr. Mann.
>>1860–1864 by Mr. Hawthorne and his family. Mr. Hawthorne died May 19, 1864.
>>1864–1868 by Mrs. Hawthorne, her two daughters and son. They went abroad in October of 1868.

1870–1873
>Owned by Abby (Mrs. George) Gray. Mr. and Mrs. Gray, with their son and daughter, occupied the house for two years.

1873–1879
>Owned and occupied by Miss Mary C. Pratt, who held here her boarding school, The Wayside Family School for Girls. It is thought that she rented the house during 1872–1873.

1879–1883
>Owned by Mr. and Mrs. George Parsons Lathrop (Rose Hawthorne), who made it their home until the death of their little son, Francis Hawthorne Lathrop, in 1881.
>>1881–1882 occupied by Mrs. Julian Hawthorne and her six children. Mr. Hawthorne returned from abroad in the spring of 1882 and rejoined his family at The Wayside.

1883–1940
>Owned by Mr. and Mrs. Daniel Lothrop and by their daughter, Miss Margaret M. Lothrop, the present owner.

(Note: The names of four other owners have been omitted. None of them lived in the house and none owned it for more than four months.)

Suggested Readings

CONCORD

History of Concord, Lemuel Shattuck, Russell, Odiorne and Company, 1835.

Incidents in the Life of Samuel Whitney . . . Memorials collected by his great-grandson, Henry Austin Whitney, 1860.

Recollections of Seventy Years, F. B. Sanborn of Concord, 2 volumes, Richard G. Badger, 1909.

Old Concord: Her Highways and Byways, Margaret Sidney, D. Lothrop Company, revised edition, 1892.

The Story of Concord Told by Concord Writers, Josephine Latham Swayne, revised edition, Meador Publishing Company, 1939.

THE ALCOTTS

Pedlar's Progress: The Life of Bronson Alcott, Odell Shepard, Little, Brown, and Company, 1937.

The Journals of Bronson Alcott, selected and edited by Odell Shepard, Little, Brown, and Company, 1938.

A. Bronson Alcott, His Life and Philosophy, F. B. Sanborn and William T. Harris, 2 volumes, Roberts Brothers, 1893.

Bronson Alcott's Fruitlands, compiled by Clara Endicott Sears, Houghton Mifflin Company, 1915.

Bronson Alcott at Alcott House, England, and Fruitlands, New England, (1842–1844), F. B. Sanborn, The Torch Press, 1908.

The Father of Little Women, Honoré Willsie Morrow, Little, Brown, and Company, 1927.

Louisa May Alcott, Her Life, Letters, and Journals, edited by Ednah D. Cheney, Roberts Brothers, 1889.

The Story of the Author of Little Women: Invincible Louisa, Cornelia Meigs, Little, Brown, and Company, 1933.

The Alcotts as I Knew Them, Clara Gowing, C. M. Clark Publishing Company, 1909.

Recollections of Louisa May Alcott, . . . Maria S. Porter, The New England Magazine Corporation, 1893.

"Louisa May Alcott" in *Portraits of American Authors*, Gamaliel Bradford, Houghton Mifflin Company, 1919.

Alcott Memoirs, Posthumously Compiled from Papers, Journals and Memoranda of the late Dr. Frederick L. H. Willis, by E. W. L. and H. B., Richard G. Badger, 1915.

May Alcott, A Memoir, Caroline Ticknor, Little, Brown, and Company, 1928.

THE HAWTHORNES

Nathaniel Hawthorne and His Wife, Julian Hawthorne, 2 volumes, James R. Osgood and Company, 1885.

Hawthorne and His Circle, Julian Hawthorne, Harper and Brothers, 1903.

The Memoirs of Julian Hawthorne, edited by his wife, Edith Garrigues Hawthorne, The Macmillan Company, 1938.

Memories of Hawthorne, Rose Hawthorne Lathrop, Houghton Mifflin and Company, 1897.

A Study of Hawthorne, George Parsons Lathrop, James R. Osgood and Company, 1876.

Romantic Rebel: The Story of Nathaniel Hawthorne, Hildegarde Hawthorne, The Century Company, 1932.

"Hawthorne," in *Yesterdays with Authors*, James T. Fields, Houghton Mifflin and Company, 1872.

Personal Recollections of Nathaniel Hawthorne, Horatio Bridge, Harper and Brothers, 1893.

Life of Nathaniel Hawthorne, Moncure D. Conway, Scribner & Welford, 1890.

Hawthorne and His Friends, F. B. Sanborn, The Torch Press, 1908.

Hawthorne and His Publisher, Caroline Ticknor, Houghton Mifflin Company, 1913.

"Hawthorne and Politics; Unpublished Letters to William B. Pike," edited by Randall Stewart, in *The New England Quarterly*, V, 237–263 (April, 1932).

"Una Hawthorne," in *Part of a Man's Life*, Thomas Wentworth Higginson, Houghton Mifflin and Company, 1906.

Letters and Journals of Thomas Wentworth Higginson, edited by Mary Thacher Higginson, Houghton Mifflin Company, 1921.

Life of Henry Wadsworth Longfellow, edited by Samuel Longfellow, 2 volumes, Ticknor and Company, 1886.

The Hawthorne Centenary at The Wayside, Concord, 1904, edited by Thomas Wentworth Higginson, Houghton Mifflin and Company, 1905.

THE LOTHROPS

" 'Margaret Sidney': The Writer of the Famous Polly Pepper Books," Norma Bright Carson, in *The Book News Monthly*, XXVIII, 407–414 (February, 1910).

"An American Publisher," Edward E. Hale, in *Lend a Hand*, IX, 253–263 (October, 1892).

Index

Agassiz, Louis, 127, 130, 138
Alcott, Abba May, 49, 132
Alcott, Amos Bronson, Part III, *passim;* 90, 101, 103–104, 106, 126, 129, 130–131, 132, 138; and Emerson, 61–63; and Thoreau, 63–64; conversations with children, 53, 62–63, 75; educational ideals and practice, 41, 43–44, 52–53, 75; interest in social reform, 41, 65–67, 68, 69–72. MSS quoted: diary, 54, 58, 60, 61–62, 63, 63–64, 64–65, 66, 70, 101, 130, 146; letter to Mrs. Hawthorne, 131
Alcott, Anna, 49, 65, 76, 100, 110, 146
Alcott, Elizabeth, 46, 47, 49, 52–53, 59, 62, 99; MS quoted: diary, 62
Alcott, Louisa May, childhood at Hillside, 46, 48, 49–50, 51, 53, 54–57, 59, 74, 76; as a poet, 55, 56, 131, 133; at Orchard House, 12, 132, 133, 183; as a war nurse, 131, 132
Alcott, Mrs. Amos Bronson, 42, 46–47, 48–49, 51, 56, 67, 68–69, 70–71, 73–75, 76, 101, 130, 132. MSS quoted: letters to her

brother, Samuel J. May, 47, 48, 49, 67, 68, 69
Alphonsa, Mother Mary. *See* Hawthorne, Rose
"Andrew Rykman's Prayer," 167
"Artist of the Beautiful," 118
Atlantic Monthly, 123, 124, 133, 135, 142

Blithedale Romance, The, 83–84
Bradford, George, 76, 110, 111
Bridge, Horatio, 85, 122, 128
Bull, Ephraim Wales, 36–37, 91–92, 126

Carlyle, Thomas, 62
Channing, William Ellery, 64–65, 138, 146
Channing, W. H. 66
Cheney, Ednah D., 56
"Chiefly about War Matters," 123
"The Child's Wish Granted," 148
Children of the American Revolution, 12, 160, 182–183
Conversations on Some of the Old Poets, 128
Conway, Moncure D., 93, 181

Daughters of the American Revolution, 183–184
"Despondency," 55
Dodge, Mary A., 129
Dolliver Romance, The, 135, 137
Duyckinck, Evert, 82, 84

Emerson, Ellen, 53, 76, 165–166, 179–180
Emerson, Mrs. Ralph Waldo, 76, 80, 115
Emerson, Ralph Waldo, 42, 61–63, 66, 100, 125, 127, 129, 130, 137, 138

Fields, James T., 118, 124, 126, 128, 134–135, 137, 142
Fields, Mrs. James T., 106, 128, 132, 133–134, 140
"Fire Worship," 7
Five Little Peppers and How They Grew, 3, 153
Five Little Peppers Grown Up, 169
Five Little Peppers Midway, 169
Flower Fables, 76
"Flutes," 133
Ford, Sophia, 73, 76
Fruitlands, 41, 67, 71

"Gail Hamilton." _See_ Dodge, Mary A.
Garrison, William Lloyd, 66
Gentle Boy, The, 104
Grapevine Cottage, 11, 23, 36, 183
Grey Champion, The, 143
Guiney, Louise Imogen , 154

Hale, Edward Everett, 154

"Happy School Days," 146
Harding, Rebecca, 129
Hassam, Childe, 154
"Hawthorne," 138
"Hawthorne and Politics," 95
Hawthorne, Beatrix, 180
Hawthorne Centenary, the, 180–181
Hawthorne, Hildegarde, 149
Hawthorne, Julian, 5, 14, 80, 87, 88, 89, 90, 91, 93, 110, 112, 115, 117–118, 120, 121, 133, 134, 144–145, 149, 180
Hawthorne, Louisa, 86–87
Hawthorne, Mrs. Nathaniel, Part IV, _passim_; interest in art, 104, 133–134; work on husband's manuscripts, 140–143. MSS quoted: diary, 87–88, 88–89, 90; letters to Mrs. Fields, 106–107, 115, 116, 132, 134, 136, 140, 141–142; letter to Mr. Fields, 142, 143
Hawthorne, Nathaniel, Part IV, _passim_; and his children, 87–88, 89–90, 93–94, 110, 114–115, 115–116, 117–118, 120–122, 123; and his friends, 84–85, 94–97, 100–101, 122, 124–125, 126–129, 130, 134–135, 138; habits of work, 86, 108, 135; illness, death, and funeral, 100, 108–109, 119, 135, 136–138. MSS quoted: letter to Evert Duyckinck, 82, 84; letter to Franklin Pierce, 85–86; letter to William D. Ticknor, 96; letter to Rose, 120–122; letter to his wife, 122;

nonsense verses, composed with his daughter Una, 123; notes for *Septimius Felton*, 125–126

Hawthorne, Rose, 6–8, 13, 80, 88, 89, 108, 110, 112, 120, 134, 144, 147, 180

"Hawthorne Tree, The," 131

Hawthorne, Una, 80, 81, 87–89, 90, 93, 97–98, 100, 103, 108, 109, 110, 111–114, 115, 120, 123, 132, 139, 143–144, 145. MSS quoted: letter to her aunt, Miss Elizabeth Palmer Peabody, 111–114; letter to Mrs. Fields, 139

Healey, George P. A., 80

Higginson, Thomas Wentworth, 80, 143–144, 181

Hillard, George S., 138, 140

Hillside, Part III. *See also* The Wayside.

Hoar, Judge Ebenezer Rockwood, 127, 138

Holmes, Dr. Oliver Wendell, 6, 124, 127, 138, 168–169

Howe, Mrs. Julia Ward, 180–181

Howe, Dr. Samuel Gridley, 66

Howells, William Dean, 128

Jewett, Sarah Orne, 154

Lane, Charles, 67–68

Lathrop, Francis Hawthorne, 147–148

Lathrop, George Parsons, 147–148

Lathrop, Mrs. George Parsons. *See* Hawthorne, Rose

Life of Henry Wadsworth Longfellow, 139

Life of Sir Walter Scott, 118

Literary Friends and Acquaintance, 128

Little Maid of Concord Town, 11–12, 184

Little Women, 48, 49, 51

Longfellow, Henry Wadsworth, 96–97, 106, 124, 127, 138, 139

Lothrop, Daniel, 3–4, 5, 153–155, 157, 159–160, 161, 163, 166, 167, 169

Lothrop, Mrs. Daniel, Part V, *passim*; 3–4, 5, 6–8, 11–12; choice of pen name, 156–157; creation of the "Pepper" family, 170–177; habits of work, 159, 177–178; historical interests, 11–12, 159–163, 182–184. MSS quoted: autobiographical data, 156–157, 158, 170–172

Louisa May Alcott, Her Life Letters and Journals, 56–57, 59

Louisa May Alcott Memorial Association, 183

Lowell, James Russell, 124, 128, 138. MS quoted: letter to Mr. Hawthorne, 128

Mann, Horace, 81, 98

Mann, Mrs. Horace, 98, 99

Marble Faun, The, 100

May, Samuel J., 58, 66, 68, 69

Memories of Hawthorne, 143

Mosses from an Old Manse, 7, 118

Mott, Mrs. Lucretia, 66

"My Kingdom," 56

"No author loves to see his books," 168

Old Concord: Her Highways and Byways, 185
Old Corner Bookstore, 126
Old North Bridge, 10, 33, 34
Orchard House, 12, 23, 99, 100, 117, 183
Our Old Home, 124
Owen, Robert, 68

Parker, Theodore, 66
Part of a Man's Life, 80
Peabody, Elizabeth Palmer, 13, 130, 165
Phelps, Elizabeth Stuart, 154
Phillips, Wendell, 66
Pierce, Franklin, 84–86, 124–125, 128, 137, 138
Pilgrim's Progress, 51
Pratt, John, 100
Prescott, Dr. Samuel, 31–32

Revere, Paul, 31

Sanborn, Frank B., 98–99, 110, 181
Saturday Club, the, 106, 127, 130
Septimius Felton, 10–11, 125–126, 135
"Sidney, Margaret." See Lothrop, Mrs. Daniel
Stewart, Randall, 95
Stone, Sidney Mason, 155–156
Study of Hawthorne, A, 91, 95
Sumner, Charles, 66, 95

Tanglewood Tales, 92–93, 95, 101
Temple School, 43, 44
Thaxter, Celia, 154
Thoreau, Henry David, 35, 44, 63–64, 125, 126, 133
Ticknor, William D., 95–96, 107, 119, 122, 136, 142

Walden Pond, 63, 64, 93
Walden Woods, 53, 62
Waverley novels, 107, 118, 119
Wayside, The, at present, 4–5; called "Hillside" by Mr. Alcott, 43, 82; called "The Wayside" by Mr. Hawthorne, 82; description of, in colonial times, 19–20; remodeled by the Alcotts, 46–49; remodeled by the Hawthornes, 101–106; remodeled by the Lothrops, 160–163; special rooms in: Hawthorne library, 106–107, 117; Hawthorne parlor, 101, 105, 162, 186; "Old Room," 19, 161–162; southeast bedroom, 47–48, 126; tower study, 101–103, 106, 146
Wayside Family School, 145–147
Week on the Concord and Merrimac Rivers, A, 63
Whittier, John Greenleaf, 6, 127, 166–168. MS quoted: 168
Whittier with the Children, 166
Wide Awake, 154, 172
Wilkins, Mary E., 154
Wonder Book, A, 84

Yesterdays with Authors, 118–119, 135, 137–138